THE SCIENCE OF
BEING WELL

Wallace D. Wattles

GENERAL PRESS

Published by

GENERAL PRESS

4805/24, Fourth Floor, Krishna House
Ansari Road, Daryaganj, New Delhi - 110002
Ph : 011-23282971, 45795759
E-mail : generalpressindia@gmail.com

www.generalpress.in

First Edition : 2022

ISBN : 9789354993893

Published by Azeem Ahmad Khan for General Press

BESTSELLING NON-FICTION

- Relativity by Albert Einstein
  Science/Physics, ISBN: 9789380914220
- Reminiscences of a Stock Operator by Edwin Lefevre
  Business/Stock Market, ISBN: 9788194764816
- Success Through a Positive Mental Attitude by Napoleon Hill
  Self-Help, ISBN: 9789390492435
- The Art of War by Sun Tzu
  Self-Help, ISBN: 9789380914893
- The Autobiography of a Yogi by Paramahansa Yogananda
  Biographies & Memoirs, ISBN: 9789380914602
- The Diary of a Young Girl by Anne Frank
  Biographies & Memoirs, ISBN: 9789380914312
- The Elements of Style by William Strunk
  Non-Fiction, ISBN: 9789389157123
- The Law of Success by Napoleon Hill
  Self-Help, ISBN: 9788180320927
- The Power of Your Subconscious Mind by Joseph Murphy
  Self-Help, ISBN: 9788180320958
- The Richest Man in Babylon by George S. Clason
  Business & Economics, ISBN: 9789387669369
- The Science of Getting Rich by Wallace D. Wattles
  Self-Help, ISBN: 9788180320972
- The World as I See It by Albert Einstein
  Non-Fiction, ISBN: 9789388118125

Search the book by its ISBN

Contents

Preface

This volume is the second of a series, the first of which is "THE SCIENCE OF GETTING RICH." As that book is intended solely for those who want money, so this is for those who want health, and who want a practical guide and handbook, not a philosophical treatise. It is an instructor in the use of the universal Principle of Life, and my effort has been to explain the way in so plain and simple a fashion that the reader, though he may have given no previous study to New Thought or metaphysics, may readily follow it to perfect health. While retaining all essentials, I have carefully eliminated all non-essentials; I have used no technical, abstruse, or difficult language, and have kept the one point in view at all times.

As its title asserts, the book deals with science, not speculation. The monistic theory of the universe—the theory that matter, mind, consciousness, and life are all manifestations of one Substance—is now accepted by most thinkers; and if you accept this theory, you cannot deny the logical conclusions you will find herein. Best of all, the methods of thought and action prescribed have been tested by the author in his own case, and in the case of hundreds of others during twelve years of practice, with continuous and unfailing success. I can say of the Science of Being Well that it works; and that wherever its laws are complied with, it can no more fail to work than the science of geometry can fail to work. If the tissues of your body have not been so destroyed that continued life is impossible, you can get well; and if you will think and act in a Certain Way, you will get well.

If the reader wishes to fully understand the monistic theory of the cosmos, he is recommended to read Hegel and Emerson; to read also "The Eternal News," a pamphlet by J. J. Brown, 300 Cathcart Road, Govanhill, Glasgow, Scotland. Some enlightenment may also be found in a series of articles by the author, which were published in *The Nautilus*, Holyoke, Mass., during the year 1909, under the title, "What Is Truth?"

Those who wish more detailed information as to the performance of the voluntary functions—eating, drinking, breathing, and sleeping—may read "New Science of Living and Healing," "Letters to a Woman's Husband," and "The Constructive Use of Foods," booklets by W. D. Wattles, which may be obtained from the publishers of this book. I would also recommend the writings of Horace Fletcher, and of Edward Hooker Dewey. Read all these, if you like, as a sort of buttress to your faith; but let me warn you against making the mistake of studying many conflicting theories, and practicing, at the same time, parts of several different "systems"; for if you get well, it must be by giving your WHOLE MIND to the *right* way of thinking and living. Remember that the SCIENCE OF BEING WELL claims to be a complete and sufficient guide in every particular. Concentrate upon the way of thinking and acting it prescribes, and follow it in every detail, and you will get well; or if you are already well, you will remain so. Trusting that you will go on until the priceless blessing of perfect health is yours, I remain,

Very truly yours,

Wallace D. Wattles.

Chapter 1

The Principle of Health

In the personal application of the Science of Being Well, as in that of the Science of Getting Rich, certain fundamental truths must be known in the beginning, and accepted without question. Some of these truths we state here:—

The perfectly natural performance of function constitutes health; and the perfectly natural performance of function results from the natural action of the Principle of Life. There is a Principle of Life in the universe; it is the One Living Substance from which all things are made. This Living Substance permeates, penetrates, and fills the interspaces of the universe; it is in and through all things, like a very refined and diffusible ether. All life comes from it; its life is all the life there is.

Man is a form of this Living Substance, and has within him a Principle of Health. (The word Principle is used as meaning source.) The Principle of Health in man, when in full constructive activity, causes all the voluntary functions of his life to be perfectly performed.

It is the Principle of Health in man which really works all healing, no matter what "system" or "remedy" is employed; and this Principle of Health is brought into Constructive Activity by thinking in a Certain Way.

I proceed now to prove this last statement. We all know that cures are wrought by all the different, and often opposite, methods employed in the various branches of the healing art. The allopath, who gives a strong dose of a counter-poison, cures his patient; and the homeopath, who gives a diminutive dose of the poison most similar to that of the disease, also cures it. If allopathy ever cured any given disease, it is certain that homeopathy never cured that disease; and if homeopathy ever cured an ailment, allopathy could not possibly cure that ailment. The two systems are radically opposite in theory and practice; and yet both "cure" most diseases. And even the remedies used by physicians in any one school are not the same. Go with a case of indigestion to half a dozen doctors, and compare their prescriptions; it is more than likely that none of the ingredients of any one of them will be in the others. Must we not conclude that their patients are healed by a Principle of Health within themselves, and not by something in the varying "remedies"?

Not only this, but we find the same ailments cured by the osteopath with manipulations of the spine; by the faith healer with prayer, by the food scientist with bills of fare, by the Christian Scientist with a formulated creed statement, by the mental scientist with affirmation, and by the hygienists with differing plans of living. What conclusion can we come to in the face of all these facts but that there is a Principle of Health which is the same in all people, and which really accomplishes all the cures; and that there is something in all the "systems" which, under favourable conditions, arouses the Principle of Health to action? That is, medicines, manipulations, prayers, bills of fare, affirmations, and hygienic practices cure whenever they cause the Principle of Health to become active; and fail whenever they do not cause it to become active. Does not all this indicate that the results depend upon the way the patient thinks about the remedy, rather than upon the ingredients in the prescription?

There is an old story which furnishes so good an illustration on this point that I will give it here. It is said that in the middle ages, the bones of a saint, kept in one of the monasteries, were working miracles of healing; on certain days a great crowd of the afflicted gathered to touch the relics, and all who did so were healed. On the eve of one of these occasions, some sacrilegious rascal gained access to the case in which the wonder-working relics were kept and stole the bones; and in the morning, with the usual crowd of sufferers waiting at the gates, the fathers found themselves shorn of the source of the miracle-working power. They resolved to keep the matter quiet, hoping that by doing so they might find the thief and recover their treasures; and hastening to the cellar of the convent they dug up the bones of a murderer, who had been buried there many years before. These they placed in the case, intending to make some plausible excuse for the failure of the saint to perform his usual miracles on that day; and then they let in the waiting assemblage of the sick and infirm. To the intense astonishment of those in the secret, the bones of the malefactor proved as efficacious as those of the saint; and the healing went on as before. One of the fathers is said to have left a history of the occurrence, in which he confessed that, in his judgment, the healing power had been in the people themselves all the time, and never in the bones at all.

Whether the story is true or not, the conclusion applies to all the cures wrought by all the systems. The Power that Heals is in the patient himself; and whether it shall become active or not does not depend upon the physical or mental means used, but upon the way the patient thinks about these means. There is a Universal Principle of Life, as Jesus taught; a great spiritual Healing Power; and there is a Principle of Health in man which is related to this Healing Power. This is dormant or active, according to the way a man thinks. He can always quicken it into activity by thinking in a Certain Way.

Your getting well does not depend upon the adoption of some system, or the finding of some remedy; people with your identical ailments have been healed by all systems and all remedies. It does not depend upon climate; some people are well and others are sick in all climates. It does not depend upon avocation, unless in case of those who work under poisonous conditions; people are well in all trades and professions. Your getting well depends upon your beginning to think—and act—in a Certain Way.

The way a man thinks about things is determined by what he believes about them. His thoughts are determined by his faith, and the results depend upon his making a personal application of his faith. If a man has faith in the efficacy of a medicine, and is able to apply that faith to himself, that medicine will certainly cause him to be cured; but though his faith be great, he will not be cured unless he applies it to himself. Many sick people have faith for others but none for themselves. So, if he has faith in a system of diet, and can personally apply that faith, it will cure him; and if he has faith in prayers and affirmations and personally applies his faith, prayers and affirmations will cure him. Faith, personally applied, cures; and no matter how great the faith or how persistent the thought, it will not cure without personal application. The Science of Being Well, then, includes the two fields of thought and action. To be well it is not enough that man should merely think in a Certain Way; he must apply his thought to himself, and he must express and externalize it in his outward life by acting in the same way that he thinks.

Chapter 2

The Foundations of Faith

Before man can think in the Certain Way which will cause his diseases to be healed, he must believe in certain truths which are here stated:—

All things are made from one Living Substance, which, in its original state, permeates, penetrates, and fills the inter-spaces of the universe. While all visible things are made from It, yet this Substance, in its first formless condition is in and through all the visible forms that It has made. Its life is in All, and its intelligence is in All.

This Substance creates by thought, and its method is by taking the form of that which it thinks about. The thought of a form held by this substance causes it to assume that form;

the thought of a motion causes it to institute that motion. Forms are created by this substance in moving itself into certain attitudes or positions. When Original Substance wishes to create a given form, it thinks of the motions which will produce that form. When it wishes to create a world, it thinks of the motions, perhaps extending through ages, which will result in its coming into the attitude and form of the world; and these motions are made. When it wishes to create an oak tree, it thinks of the sequences of movement, perhaps extending through ages, which will result in the form of an oak tree; and these motions are made. The particular sequences of motion by which differing forms should be produced were established in the beginning; they are changeless. Certain motions instituted in the Formless Substance will forever produce certain forms.

Man's body is formed from the Original Substance, and is the result of certain motions, which first existed as thoughts of Original Substance. The motions which produce, renew, and repair the body of man are called functions, and these functions are of two classes: voluntary and involuntary. The involuntary functions are under the control of the Principle of Health in man, and are performed in a perfectly healthy manner so long as man thinks in a certain way. The voluntary functions of life are eating, drinking, breathing, and sleeping. These, entirely or in part, are under the direction of man's conscious mind; and he can perform them in a perfectly healthy way if he will. If he does not perform them in a healthy way, he cannot long be well. So we see that if man thinks in a certain way, and eats, drinks, breathes, and sleeps in a corresponding way, he will be well.

The involuntary functions of man's life are under the direct control of the Principle of Health, and so long as man thinks in a perfectly healthy way, these functions are perfectly performed; for the action of the Principle of Health is largely directed by man's conscious thought, affecting his sub-conscious mind.

Man is a thinking center, capable of originating thought; and as he does not know everything, he makes mistakes and thinks error. Not knowing everything, he believes things to be true which are not true. Man holds in his thought the idea of diseased and abnormal functioning and conditions, and so perverts the action of the Principle of Health, causing diseased and abnormal functioning and conditions within his own body. In the Original Substance there are held only the thoughts of perfect motion; perfect and healthy function; complete life. God never thinks disease or imperfection. But for countless ages men have held thoughts of disease, abnormality, old age, and death; and the perverted functioning resulting from these thoughts has become a part of the inheritance of the race. Our ancestors have, for many generations, held imperfect ideas concerning human form and functioning; and we begin life with racial sub-conscious impressions of imperfection and disease.

This is not natural, or a part of the plan of nature. The purpose of nature can be nothing else than the perfection of life. This we see from the very nature of life itself. It is the nature of life to continually advance toward more perfect living;

advancement is the inevitable result of the very act of living. Increase is always the result of active living; whatever lives must live more and more. The seed, lying in the granary, has life, but it is not living. Put it into the soil and it becomes active, and at once begins to gather to itself from the surrounding substance, and to build a plant form. It will so cause increase that a seed head will be produced containing thirty, sixty, or a hundred seeds, each having as much life as the first.

Life, by living, increases.

Life cannot live without increasing, and the fundamental impulse of life is to live. It is in response to this fundamental impulse that Original Substance works, and creates. God must live; and he cannot live except as he creates and increases. In multiplying forms, He is moving on to live more.

The universe is a Great Advancing Life, and the purpose of nature is the advancement of life toward perfection; toward perfect functioning. The purpose of nature is perfect health.

The purpose of Nature, so far as man is concerned, is that he should be continuously advancing into more life, and progressing toward perfect life; and that he should live the most complete life possible in his present sphere of action.

This must be so, because That which lives in man is seeking more life.

Give a little child a pencil and paper, and he begins to draw crude figures; That which lives in him is trying to express Itself in art. Give him a set of blocks, and he will try to build something; That which lives in him is seeking expression in architecture. Seat him at a piano, and he will try to draw harmony from the keys; That which lives in him is trying to express Itself in music. That which lives in man is always seeking to live more; and since man lives most when he is well, the Principle of Nature in him can seek only health. The natural state of man is a state of perfect health; and everything in him, and in nature, tends toward health.

Sickness can have no place in the thought of Original Substance, for it is by its own nature continually impelled toward the fullest and most perfect life; therefore, toward health. Man, as he exists in the thought of the Formless Substance, has perfect health. Disease, which is abnormal or perverted function—motion imperfectly made, or made in the direction of imperfect life—has no place in the thought of the Thinking Stuff.

The Supreme Mind never thinks of disease. Disease was not created or ordained by God, or sent forth from him. It is wholly a product of separate consciousness; of the individual thought of man. God, the Formless Substance, does not see disease, think disease, know disease, or recognize disease. Disease is recognized only by the thought of man; God thinks nothing but health.

From all the foregoing, we see that health is *a fact* or TRUTH in the original substance from which we are all formed; and that disease is imperfect functioning, resulting from the imperfect thoughts of men, past and present. If man's thoughts of himself had always been those of perfect health, man could not possibly now be otherwise than perfectly healthy.

Man in perfect health is the thought of Original Substance, and man in imperfect health is the result of his own failure to think perfect health, and to perform the voluntary functions of life in a healthy way. We will here arrange in a syllabus the basic truths of the Science of Being Well:—

There is a Thinking Substance from which all things are made, and which, in its original state, permeates, penetrates, and fills the interspaces of the universe. It is the life of All.

The thought of a form in this Substance causes the form; the thought of a motion produces the motion. In relation to man, the thoughts of this Substance are always of perfect functioning and perfect health.

Man is a thinking center, capable of original thought; and his thought has power over his own functioning. By thinking imperfect thoughts he has caused imperfect and perverted functioning; and by performing the voluntary functions of life in a perverted manner, he has assisted in causing disease.

If man will think only thoughts of perfect health, he can cause within himself the functioning of perfect health; all the Power of Life will be exerted to assist him. But this healthy functioning will not continue unless man performs the external, or voluntary, functions of living in a healthy manner.

Man's first step must be to learn how to think perfect health; and his second step to learn how to eat, drink, breathe, and sleep in a perfectly healthy way. If man takes these two steps, he will certainly become well, and remain so.

Chapter 3

Life and Its Organisms

The human body is the abiding place of an energy which renews it when worn; which eliminates waste or poisonous matter, and which repairs the body when broken or injured. This energy we call life. Life is not generated or produced within the body; *it produces the body.*

The seed which has been kept in the storehouse for years will grow when planted in the soil; it will produce a plant. But the life in the plant is not generated by its growing; it is the life which makes the plant grow.

The performance of function does not cause life; it is life which causes function to be performed. Life is first; function afterward.

It is life which distinguishes organic from inorganic matter, but it is not produced after the organization of matter.

Life is the principle or force which causes organization; it builds organisms.

It is a principle or force inherent in Original Substance; all life is One.

This Life Principle of the All is the Principle of Health in man, and becomes constructively active whenever man thinks in a certain way. Whoever, therefore, thinks in this Certain Way will surely have perfect health if his external functioning is in conformity with his thought. But the external functioning must conform to the thought; man cannot hope to be well by thinking health, if he eats, drinks, breathes, and sleeps like a sick man.

The universal Life Principle, then, is the Principle of Health in man. It is one with original substance. There is one Original Substance from which all things are made; this substance is alive, and its life is the Principle of Life of the universe. This Substance has created from itself all the forms of organic life by thinking them, or by thinking the motions and functions which produce them.

Original Substance thinks only health, because It knows all truth; there is no truth which is not known in the Formless, which is All, and in all. It not only knows all truth, but it has all power; its vital power is the source of all the energy there is. A conscious life which knows all truth and which has all power cannot go wrong or perform function imperfectly; knowing all, it knows, too much to go wrong, and so the Formless cannot be diseased or think disease.

Man is a form of this original substance, and has a separate consciousness of his own; but his consciousness is limited, and therefore imperfect. By reason of his limited knowledge man can and does think wrongly, and so he causes perverted and imperfect functioning in his own body. Man has not known too much to go wrong. The diseased or imperfect functioning may not instantly result from an imperfect thought, but it is bound to come if the thought becomes habitual. Any thought continuously held by man tends to the establishment of the corresponding condition in his body.

Also, man has failed to learn how to perform the voluntary functions of his life in a healthy way. He does not know when, what, and how to eat; he knows little about breathing, and less about sleep. He does all these things in a wrong way, and under wrong conditions; and this because he has neglected to follow the only sure guide to the knowledge of life. He has tried to live by logic rather than by instinct; he has made living a matter of art, and not of nature. And he has gone wrong.

His only remedy is to begin to go right; and this he can surely do. It is the work of this book to teach the whole truth, so that the man who reads it shall know too much to go wrong.

The thoughts of disease produce the forms of disease. Man must learn to think health; and being Original Substance which takes the form of its thoughts, he will become the form of health and manifest perfect health in all his functioning. The people who were healed by touching the bones of the saint were really healed by thinking in a certain way, and not by any power emanating from the relics. There is no healing power in the bones of dead men, whether they be those of saint or sinner.

The people who were healed by the doses of either the allopath or the homeopath were also really healed by thinking in a certain way; there is no drug which has within itself the power to heal disease.

The people who have been healed by prayers and affirmations were also healed by thinking in a certain way; there is no curative power in strings of words.

All the sick who have been healed, by whatsoever "system," have thought in a certain way; and a little examination will show us what this way is.

The two essentials of the Way are Faith, and a Personal Application of the Faith.

The people who touched the saint's bones had faith; and so great was their faith that in the instant they touched the relics they SEVERED ALL MENTAL RELATIONS WITH DISEASE, AND MENTALLY UNIFIED THEMSELVES WITH HEALTH.

This change of mind was accompanied by an intense devotional FEELING which penetrated to the deepest recesses of their souls, and so aroused the Principle of Health to powerful action. By faith they claimed that they were healed, or appropriated health to themselves; and in full faith they ceased to think of themselves in connection with disease and thought of themselves only in connection with health.

These are the two essentials to thinking in the Certain Way which will make you well: first, claim or appropriate health by faith; and, second, sever all mental relations with disease, and enter into mental relations with health. That which we make ourselves, mentally, we become physically; and that with which we unite ourselves mentally we become unified with physically. If your thought always relates you to disease, then your thought becomes a fixed power to cause disease within you; and if your thought always relates you to health, then your thought becomes a fixed power exerted to keep you well.

In the case of the people who are healed by medicines, the result is obtained in the same way. They have, consciously or unconsciously, sufficient faith in the means used to cause them to sever mental relations with disease and enter into mental relations with health. Faith may be unconscious. It is possible for us to have a sub-conscious or inbred faith in things like medicine, in which we do not believe to any extent objectively; and this sub-conscious faith may be quite sufficient to quicken the Principle of Health into constructive activity. Many who have little conscious faith are healed in this way; while many others who have great faith in the means are not healed because they do not make the personal application to themselves; their faith is general, but not specific for their own cases.

In the Science of Being Well we have two main points to consider: first, how to think with faith; and, second, how to so apply the thought to ourselves as to quicken the Principle of Health into constructive activity. We begin by learning What to Think.

Chapter 4

What to Think

In order to sever all mental relations with disease, you must enter into mental relations with health, making the process positive not negative; one of assumption, not of rejection. You are to receive or appropriate health rather than to reject and deny disease. Denying disease accomplishes next to nothing; it does little good to cast out the devil and leave the house vacant, for he will presently return with others worse than himself. When you enter into full and constant mental relations with health, you must of necessity cease all relationship with disease. The first step in the Science of Being Well is, then, to enter into complete thought connection with health.

The best way to do this is to form a mental image or picture of yourself as being well, imagining a perfectly strong and healthy body; and to spend sufficient time in contemplating this image to make it your habitual thought of yourself.

This is not so easy as it sounds; it necessitates the taking of considerable time for meditation, and not all persons have the imaging faculty well enough developed to form a distinct mental picture of themselves in a perfect or idealized body. It is much easier, as in "The Science of Getting Rich," to form a mental image of the things one wants to have; for we have seen these things, or their counterparts, and know how they look; we can picture them very easily from memory. But we have never seen ourselves in a perfect body, and a *clear* mental image is hard to form.

It is not necessary or essential, however, to have a clear mental image of yourself as you wish to be; it is only essential to form a CONCEPTION of perfect health, and to relate yourself to it. This Conception of Health is not a mental picture of a particular thing; it is an understanding of health, and carries with it the idea of perfect functioning in every part and organ.

You may TRY to picture yourself as perfect in physique; that helps; and you MUST *think of yourself as doing everything in the manner of a perfectly strong and healthy person.* You can picture yourself as walking down the street with an erect body and a vigorous stride; you can picture yourself as doing your day's work easily and with surplus vigor, never tired or weak; you can picture in your mind how all things would be done by a person full of health and power, and you can make yourself the central figure in the picture, doing things in just that way. Never think of the ways in which weak or sickly people do things; always think of the way strong people do things. Spend your leisure time in thinking about the Strong Way, until you have a good conception of it; and always think of yourself in connection with the Strong Way of Doing Things. That is what I mean by having a Conception of Health.

In order to establish perfect functioning in every part, man does not have to study anatomy or physiology, so that he can form a mental image of each separate organ and address himself to it. He does not have to "treat" his liver, his kidneys, his stomach, or his heart. There is one Principle of Health in man, which has control over all the involuntary functions of his life; and the thought of perfect health, impressed upon this Principle, will reach each part and organ. Man's liver is not controlled by a liver-principle, his stomach by a digestive principle, and so on; the Principle of Health is One.

The less you go into the detailed study of physiology, the better for you. Our knowledge of this science is very imperfect, and leads to imperfect thought. Imperfect thought causes imperfect functioning, which is disease. Let me illustrate: Until quite recently, physiology fixed ten days as the extreme limit of man's endurance without food; it was considered that only in exceptional cases could he survive a longer fast. So the impression became universally disseminated that one who was deprived of food must die in from five to ten days; and numbers of people, when cut off from food by shipwreck, accident, or famine, did die within this period. But the performances of Dr. Tanner, the forty-day faster, and the writings of Dr. Dewey and others on the fasting cure, together with the experiments of numberless people who have fasted from forty to sixty days, have shown that man's ability to live without food is vastly greater than had been supposed. Any person, properly educated, can fast from twenty to forty days with little loss in weight, and often with no apparent loss of strength at all. The people who starved to death in ten days or less did so because they believed that death was inevitable; an erroneous physiology had given them a wrong thought about themselves. When a man is deprived of food he will die in from ten to fifty days, according to the way he has been taught; or, in other words, according to the way he thinks about it. So you see that an erroneous physiology can work very mischievous results.

No Science of Being Well can be founded on current physiology; it is not sufficiently exact in its knowledge. With all its pretensions, comparatively little is really known as to the interior workings and processes of the body. It is not known just how food is digested; it is not known just what part food plays, if any, in the generation of force. It is not known exactly what the liver, spleen, and pancreas are for, or what part their secretions play in the chemistry of assimilation. On all these and most other points we theorize, but we do not really know. When man begins to study physiology, he enters the domain of theory and disputation; he comes among conflicting opinions, and he is bound to form mistaken ideas concerning himself. These mistaken ideas lead to the thinking of wrong thoughts, and this leads to perverted functioning and disease. All that the most perfect knowledge of physiology could do for man would be to enable him to think only thoughts of perfect health, and to eat, drink, breathe, and sleep in a perfectly healthy way; and this, as we shall show, he can do without studying physiology at all.

This, for the most part, is true of all hygiene. There are certain fundamental propositions which we should know; and these will be explained in later chapters, but aside from these propositions, ignore physiology and hygiene. They tend to fill your mind with thoughts of imperfect conditions, and these thoughts will produce the imperfect conditions in your own body. You cannot study any "science" which recognizes disease, if you are to think nothing but health.

Drop all investigation as to your present condition, its causes, or possible results, and set yourself to the work of forming a conception of health.

Think about health and the possibilities of health; of the work that may be done and the pleasures that may be enjoyed in a condition of perfect health. Then make this conception your guide in thinking of yourself; refuse to entertain for an instant any thought of yourself which is not in harmony with it. When any idea of disease or imperfect functioning enters your mind, cast it out instantly by calling up a thought which is in harmony with the Conception of Health.

Think of yourself at all times as realizing conception; as being a strong and perfectly healthy personage; and do not harbor a contrary thought.

KNOW that as you think of yourself in unity with this conception, the Original Substance which permeates and fills the tissues of your body is taking form according to the thought; and know that this Intelligent Substance or mind stuff will cause function to be performed in such a way that your body will be rebuilt with perfectly healthy cells.

The Intelligent Substance, from which all things are made, permeates and penetrates all things; and so it is in and through your body. It moves according to its thoughts; and so if you hold only the thoughts of perfectly healthy function, it will cause the movements of perfectly healthy function within you.

Hold with persistence to the thought of perfect health in relation to yourself; do not permit yourself to think in any other way. Hold this thought with perfect faith that it is the fact, the truth. It is the truth so far as your mental body is concerned. You have a mind-body and a physical body; the mind-body takes form just as you think of yourself, and any thought which you hold continuously is made visible by the transformation of the physical body into its image. Implanting the thought of perfect functioning in the mind-body will, in due time, cause perfect functioning in the physical body.

The transformation of the physical body into the image of the ideal held by the mind-body is not accomplished instantaneously; we cannot transfigure our physical bodies at will as Jesus did. In the creation and recreation of forms, Substance moves along the fixed lines of growth it has established; and the impression upon it of the health thought causes the healthy body to be built cell by cell. Holding only thoughts of perfect health will ultimately cause perfect functioning; and perfect functioning will in due time produce a perfectly healthy body. It may be as well to condense this chapter into a syllabus:—

Your physical body is permeated and fitted with an Intelligent Substance, which forms a body of mind-stuff. This mind-stuff controls the functioning of your physical body.

A thought of disease or of imperfect function, impressed upon the mind-stuff, causes disease or imperfect functioning in the physical body. If you are diseased, it is because wrong thoughts have made impressions on this mind-stuff; these may have been either your own thoughts or those of your parents; we begin life with many sub-conscious impressions, both right and wrong. But the natural tendency of all mind is toward health, and if no thoughts are held in the conscious mind save those of health, all internal functioning will come to be performed in a perfectly healthy manner.

The Power of Nature within you is sufficient to overcome all hereditary impressions, and if you will learn to control your thoughts, so that you shall think only those of health, and if you will perform the voluntary functions of life in a perfectly healthy way, you can certainly be well.

Chapter 5

Faith

The Principle of Health is moved by Faith; nothing else can call it into action, and only faith can enable you to relate yourself to health, and sever your relation with disease, in your thoughts.

You will continue to think of disease unless you have faith in health. If you do not have faith you will doubt; if you doubt, you will fear; and if you fear, you will relate yourself in mind to that which you fear.

If you fear disease, you will think of yourself in connection with disease; and that will produce within yourself the form and motions of disease. Just as Original Substance creates from itself the forms of its thoughts, so your mind-body, which is original substance, takes the form and motion of whatever you think about. If you fear disease, dread disease, have doubts about your safety from disease, or if you even contemplate disease, you will connect yourself with it and create its forms and motions within you.

Let me enlarge somewhat upon this point. The potency, or creative power, of a thought is given to it *by the faith that is in it.*

Thoughts which contain no faith create no forms.

The Formless Substance, which knows all truth and therefore thinks only truth, has perfect faith in every thought, because it thinks only truth; and so all its thoughts create.

But if you will imagine a thought in Formless Substance in which there was no faith, you will see that such a thought could not cause the Substance to move or take form.

Keep in mind the fact that only those thoughts which are conceived in faith have creative energy. Only those thoughts which have faith with them are able to change function, or to quicken the Principle of Health into activity.

If you do not have faith in health, you will certainly have faith in disease. If you do not have faith in health, it will do you no good to think about health, for your thoughts will have no potency, and will cause no change for the better in your conditions. If you do not have faith in health, I repeat, you will have faith in disease; and if, under such conditions, you think about health for ten hours a day, and think about disease for only a few minutes, the disease thought will control your condition because it will have the potency of faith, while the health thought will not. Your mind-body will take on the form and motions of disease and retain them, because your health thought will not have sufficient dynamic force to change form or motion.

In order to practice the Science of Being Well, you must have complete faith in health.

Faith begins in belief; and we now come to the question: *What must you believe in order to have faith in health?*

You must believe that there is more health-power than disease-power in both yourself and your environment; and you cannot help believing this if you consider the facts. These are the facts:—

> *There is a Thinking Substance from which all things are made, and which, in its original state, permeates, penetrates, and fills the interspaces of the universe.*
>
> *The thought of a form, in this Substance, produces the form; the thought of a motion institutes the motion. In relation to man, the thoughts of Original Substance are always of perfect health and perfect functioning. This Substance, within and without man, always exerts its power toward health.*
>
> *Man is a thinking center, capable of original thought. He has a mind-body of Original Substance permeating a physical body; and the functioning of his physical body is determined by the FAITH of his mind-body. If man thinks with faith of the functioning of health, he will cause his internal functions to be performed in a healthy manner, provided that he performs the external functions in a corresponding manner. But if man thinks, with faith, of disease, or of the power of disease, he will cause his internal functioning to be the functioning of disease.*

The Original Intelligent Substance is in man, moving toward health; and it is pressing upon him from every side. Man lives, moves, and has his being in a limitless ocean of health-power; and he uses this power according to his faith. If he appropriates it and applies it to himself it is all his; and if he unifies himself with it by unquestioning faith, he cannot fail to attain health, for the power of this Substance is all the power there is.

A belief in the above statements is a foundation for faith in health. If you believe them, you believe that health is the natural state of man, and that man lives in the midst of Universal Health; that all the power of nature makes for health, and that health is possible to all, and can surely be attained by all. You will believe that the power of health in the universe is ten thousand times greater than that of disease; in fact, that disease has no power whatever, being only the result of perverted thought and faith. And if you believe that health is possible to you, and that it may surely be attained by you, and that you know exactly what to do in order to attain it, you will have faith in health. You will have this faith and knowledge if you read this book through with care and determine to believe in and practice its teachings.

It is not merely the possession of faith, but the personal application of faith which works healing. You must claim health in the beginning, and form a conception of health, and, as far as may be, of yourself as a perfectly healthy person; and then, by faith, you must claim that you ARE REALIZING this conception.

Do not assert with faith that you are going to get well; assert with faith that you ARE well.

Having faith in health, and applying it to yourself, means having faith that you are healthy; *and the first step in this is to claim that it is the truth.*

Mentally take the attitude of being well, and do not say anything or do anything which contradicts this attitude. Never speak a word or assume a physical attitude which does not harmonize with the claim: "I am perfectly well." When you walk, go with a brisk step, and with your chest thrown out and your head held up; watch that at all times your physical actions and attitudes are those of a healthy person. When you find that you have relapsed into the attitude of weakness or disease, change instantly; straighten up; think of health and power. Refuse to consider yourself as other than a perfectly healthy person.

One great aid—perhaps the greatest aid—in applying your faith you will find in the exercise of gratitude.

Whenever you think of yourself, or of your advancing condition, give thanks to the Great Intelligent Substance for the perfect health you are enjoying.

Remember that, as Swedenborg taught, there is a continual inflow of life from the Supreme, which is received by all created things according to their forms; and by man according to his faith. Health from God is continually being urged upon you; and when you think of this, lift up your mind reverently to Him, and give thanks that you have been led to the Truth and into perfect health of mind and body. Be, all the time, in a grateful frame of mind, and let gratitude be evident in your speech.

Gratitude will help you to own and control your own field of thought.

Whenever the thought of disease is presented to you, instantly claim health, and thank God for the perfect health you have. Do this so that there shall be no room in your mind for a thought of ill. Every thought connected in any way with ill health is unwelcome, and you can close the door of your mind in its face by asserting that you are well, and by reverently thanking God that it is so. Soon the old thoughts will return no more.

Gratitude has a twofold effect; it strengthens your own faith, and it brings you into close and harmonious relations with the Supreme. You believe that there is one Intelligent Substance from which all life and all power come; you believe that you receive your own life from this substance; and you relate yourself closely to It by feeling continuous gratitude. It is easy to see that the more closely you relate yourself to the Source of Life the more readily you may receive life from it; and it is easy also to see that your relation to It is a matter of mental attitude. We cannot come into physical relationship with God, for God is mind-stuff and we also are mind-stuff; our relation with Him must therefore be a mind relation. It is plain, then, that the man who feels deep and hearty gratitude will live in closer touch with God than the man who never looks up to Him in thankfulness. The ungrateful or unthankful mind really denies that it receives at all, and so cuts its connection with the Supreme. The grateful mind is always looking toward the Supreme, and is always open to receive from it; and it will receive continually.

> *The Principle of Health in man receives its vital power from the Principle of Life in the universe; and man relates himself to the Principle of Life by faith in health, and by gratitude for the health he receives.*
>
> *Man may cultivate both faith and gratitude by the proper use of his will.*

Chapter 6

Use of the Will

In the practice of the Science of Being Well the will is not used to compel yourself to go when you are not really able to go, or to do things when you are not physically strong enough to do them. You do not direct your will upon your physical body or try to compel the proper performance of internal function by will power.

You direct the will upon the mind, and use it in determining what you shall believe, what you shall think, and to what you shall give your attention.

The will should never be used upon any person or thing external to you, and it should never be used upon your own body. The sole legitimate use of the will is in determining to what you shall give your attention, and what you shall think about the things to which your attention is given.

All belief begins in the will to believe.

You cannot always and instantly believe what you will to believe; but you can always will to believe what you want to believe. You want to believe truth about health, and you can will to do so. The statements you have been reading in this book are the truth about health, and you can will to believe them; this must be your first step toward getting well.

These are the statements you must will to believe:—

> *That there is a Thinking Substance from which all things are made, and that man receives the Principle of Health, which is his life, from this Substance.*
>
> *That man himself is Thinking Substance; a mind-body, permeating a physical body, and that as man's thoughts are, so will the functioning of his physical body be.*
>
> *That if man will think only thoughts of perfect health, he must and will cause the internal and involuntary functioning of his body to be the functioning of health, provided that his external and voluntary functioning and attitude are in accordance with his thoughts.*

When you will to believe these statements, you must also begin to act upon them. You cannot long retain a belief unless you act upon it; you cannot increase a belief until it becomes faith unless you act upon it; and you certainly cannot expect to reap benefits in any way from a belief so long as you act as if the opposite were true. You cannot long have faith in health if you continue to act like a sick person. If you continue to act like a sick person, you cannot help continuing to think of yourself as a sick person; and if you continue to think of yourself as a sick person, you will continue to be a sick person.

The first step toward acting externally like a well person is to begin to act internally like a well person. Form your conception of perfect health, and get into the way of thinking about perfect health until it begins to have a definite meaning to you. Picture yourself as doing the things a strong and healthy person would do, and have faith that you can and will do those things in that way; continue this until you have a vivid CONCEPTION of health, and what it means to you. When I speak in this book of a conception of health, I mean a conception that carries with it the idea of the way a healthy person looks and does things. Think of yourself in connection with health until you form a conception of how you would live, appear, act, and do things as a perfectly healthy person. Think about yourself in connection with health until you conceive of yourself, in imagination, as always doing everything in the manner of a well person; until the thought of health conveys the idea of what health means to you. As I have said in a former chapter, you may not be able to form a clear mental image of yourself in perfect health, but you can form a conception of yourself as acting like a healthy person.

Form this conception, and then think only thoughts of perfect health in relation to yourself, and, so far as may be possible, in relation to others. When a thought of sickness or disease is presented to you, reject it; do not let it get into your mind; do not entertain or consider it at all. Meet it by thinking health; by thinking that you are well, and by being sincerely grateful for the health you are receiving. Whenever suggestions of disease are coming thick and fast upon you, and you are in a "tight place," fall back upon the exercise of gratitude. Connect yourself with the Supreme; give thanks to God for the perfect health He gives you, and you will soon find yourself able to control your thoughts, and to think what you want to think. In times of doubt, trial, and temptation, the exercise of gratitude is always a sheet anchor which will prevent you from being swept away. Remember that the great essential thing is to SEVER ALL MENTAL RELATIONS WITH DISEASE, AND TO ENTER INTO FULL MENTAL RELATIONSHIP WITH HEALTH. This is the KEY to all mental healing; it is the whole thing. Here we see the secret of the great success of Christian Science; more than any other formulated system of practice, it insists that its converts shall sever relations with disease, and relate themselves fully with health. The healing power of Christian Science is not in its theological formulæ, nor in its denial of matter; but in the fact that it induces the sick to ignore disease as an unreal thing and accept health by faith as a reality. Its failures are made because its practitioners, while thinking in the Certain Way, do not eat, drink, breathe, and sleep in the same way.

While there is no healing power in the repetition of strings of words, yet it is a very convenient thing to have the central thoughts so formulated that you can repeat them readily, so that you can use them as affirmations whenever you are surrounded by an environment which gives you adverse suggestions. When those around you begin to talk of sickness and death, close your ears and mentally assert something like the following:—

There is One Substance, and I am that Substance.

That Substance is eternal, and it is Life; I am that Substance, and I am Eternal Life.

That Substance knows no disease; I am that Substance, and I am Health.

Exercise your will power in choosing only those thoughts which are thoughts of health, and arrange your environment so that it shall suggest thoughts of health. Do not have about you books, pictures, or other things which suggest death, disease, deformity, weakness, or age; have only those which convey the ideas of health, power, joy, vitality, and youth. When you are confronted with a book, or anything else which suggests disease, do not give it your attention. Think of your conception of health, and your gratitude, and affirm as above; use your will power to fix your attention upon thoughts of health. In a future chapter I shall touch upon this point again; what I wish to make plain here is that you must think only health, recognize only health, and give your attention only to health; and that you must control thought, recognition, and attention by the use of your will.

Do not try to use your will to compel the healthy performance of function within you. The Principle of Health will attend to that, if you give your attention only to thoughts of health.

Do not try to exert your will upon the Formless to compel It to give you more vitality or power; it is already placing all the power there is at your service.

You do not have to use your will to conquer adverse conditions, or to subdue unfriendly forces; there are no unfriendly forces; there is only One Force, and that force is friendly to you; it is a force which makes for health.

Everything in the universe wants you to be well; you have absolutely nothing to overcome but your own habit of thinking in a certain way about disease, and you can do this only by forming a habit of thinking in another Certain Way about health.

Man can cause all the internal functions of his body to be performed in a perfectly healthy manner by continuously thinking in a Certain Way, and by performing the external functions in a certain way.

He can think in this Certain Way by controlling his attention, and he can control his attention by the use of his will.

He can decide what things he will think about.

Chapter 7

Health from God

I will give a chapter here to explaining how man may receive health from the Supreme. By the Supreme I mean the Thinking Substance from which all things are made, and which is in all and through all, seeking more complete expression and fuller life. This Intelligent Substance, in a perfectly fluid state, permeates and penetrates all things, and is in touch with all minds. It is the source of all energy and power, and constitutes the "inflow" of life which Swedenborg saw, vitalizing all things. It is working to one definite end, and for the fulfillment of one purpose; and that purpose is the advancement of life toward the complete expression of Mind. When man harmonizes himself with this Intelligence, it can and will give him health and wisdom. When man holds steadily to the purpose to live more abundantly, he comes into harmony with this Supreme Intelligence.

The purpose of the Supreme Intelligence is the most Abundant Life for all; the purpose of this Supreme Intelligence for you is that you should live more abundantly. If, then, your own purpose is to live more abundantly, you are unified with the Supreme; you are working with It, and it must work with you. But as the Supreme Intelligence is in all, *if you harmonize with it you must harmonize with all; and you must desire more abundant life for all as well as for yourself.* Two great benefits come to you from being in harmony with the Supreme Intelligence.

First, you will receive wisdom. By wisdom I do not mean knowledge of facts so much as ability to perceive and understand facts, and to judge soundly and act rightly in all matters relating to life. Wisdom is the power to perceive truth, and the ability to make the best use of the knowledge of truth. It is the power to perceive at once the best end to aim at, and the means best adapted to attain that end. With wisdom comes poise, and the power to think rightly; to control and guide your thoughts, and to avoid the difficulties which come from wrong thinking. With wisdom you will be able to select the right courses for your particular needs, and to so govern yourself in all ways as to secure the best results. You will know how to do what you want to do. You can readily see that wisdom must be an essential attribute of the Supreme Intelligence, since That which knows all truth must be wise; and you can also see that just in proportion as you harmonize and unify your mind with that Intelligence you will have wisdom.

But I repeat that since this Intelligence is All, and in all, you can enter into Its wisdom only by harmonizing with all.

If there is anything in your desires or your purpose which will bring oppression to any, or work injustice to, or cause lack of life for any, you cannot receive wisdom from the Supreme. Furthermore, your purpose for your own self must be the best.

Man can live in three general ways: for the gratification of his body, for that of his intellect, or for that of his soul. The first is accomplished by satisfying the desires for food, drink, and those other things which give enjoyable physical sensations. The second is accomplished by doing those things which cause pleasant mental sensations, such as gratifying the desire for knowledge or those for fine clothing, fame, power, and so on. The third is accomplished by giving way to the instincts of unselfish love and altruism. Man lives most wisely and completely when he functions most perfectly along all of these lines, without excess in any of them. The man who lives swinishly, for the body alone, is unwise and out of harmony with God; that man who lives solely for the cold enjoyments of the intellect, though he be absolutely moral, is unwise and out of harmony with God; and the man who lives wholly for the practice of altruism, and who throws himself away for others, is as unwise and as far from harmony with God as those who go to excess in other ways.

To come into full harmony with the Supreme, you must purpose to LIVE; to live to the utmost of your capabilities in body, mind, and soul. This must mean the full exercise of function in all the different ways, but without excess; for excess in one causes deficiency in the others. Behind your desire for health is your own desire for more abundant life; and behind that is the desire of the Formless Intelligence to live more fully in you. So, as you advance toward perfect health, hold steadily to the purpose to attain complete life, physical, mental, and spiritual; to advance in all ways, and in every way to live more; if you hold this purpose you will be given wisdom. "He that willeth to do the will of the Father shall KNOW," said Jesus. Wisdom is the most desirable gift that can come to man, for it makes him rightly self-governing.

But wisdom is not all you may receive from the Supreme Intelligence; you may receive physical energy, vitality, life force. The energy of the Formless Substance is unlimited, and permeates everything; you are already receiving or appropriating to yourself this energy in an automatic and instinctive way, but you can do so to a far greater degree if you set about it intelligently. The measure of a man's strength is not what God is willing to give him, but what he, himself, has the will and the intelligence to appropriate to himself. God gives you all there is; your only question is how much to take of the unlimited supply.

Professor James has pointed out that there is apparently no limit to the powers of men; and this is simply because man's power comes from the inexhaustible reservoir of the Supreme. The runner who has reached the stage of exhaustion, when his physical power seems entirely gone, by running on in a Certain Way may receive his "second wind"; his strength is renewed in a seemingly miraculous fashion, and he can go on indefinitely. And by continuing in the Certain Way, he may receive a third, fourth, and fifth "wind"; we do not know where the limit is, or how far it may be possible to extend it. The conditions are that the runner must have absolute faith that the strength will come;

that he must think steadily of strength, and have perfect confidence that he has it, and that he must continue to run on. If he admits a doubt into his mind, he falls exhausted, and if he stops running to wait for the accession of strength, it will never come. His faith in strength, his faith that he *can* keep on running, his unwavering purpose *to* keep on running, and his action *in* keeping on seem to connect him to the source of energy in such a way as to bring him a new supply.

In a very similar manner, the sick person who has unquestioning faith in health, whose purpose brings him into harmony with the source, and who performs the voluntary functions of life in a certain way, will receive vital energy sufficient for all his needs, and for the healing of all his diseases. God, who seeks to live and express himself fully in man, delights to give man all that is needed for the most abundant life. Action and reaction are equal, and when you desire to live more, if you are in mental harmony with the Supreme, the forces which make for life begin to concentrate about you and upon you. The One Life begins to move toward you, and your environment becomes surcharged with it. Then, if you appropriate it by faith, it is yours. "Ye shall ask what ye will, and it shall be done unto you." Your Father giveth not his spirit by measure; he delights to give good gifts to you.

Chapter 8

Summary of the Mental Actions

Let me now summarize the mental actions and attitudes necessary to the practice of the Science of Being Well: first, you believe that there is a Thinking Substance, from which all things are made, and which, in its original state, permeates, penetrates, and fills the interspaces of the universe. This Substance is the Life of All, and is seeking to express more life in all. It is the Principle of Life of the universe, and the Principle of Health in man.

Man is a form of this Substance, and draws his vitality from it; he is a mind-body of original substance, permeating a physical body, and the thoughts of his mind-body control the functioning of his physical body. If man thinks no thoughts save those of perfect health, the functions of his physical body will be performed in a manner of perfect health.

If you would consciously relate yourself to the All-Health, your purpose must be to live fully on every plane of your being. You must want all that there is in life for body, mind, and soul; and this will bring you into harmony with all the life there is. The person who is in conscious and intelligent harmony with All will receive a continuous inflow of vital power from the Supreme Life; and this inflow is prevented by angry, selfish or antagonistic mental attitudes. If you are against any part, you have severed relations with all; you will receive life, but only instinctively and automatically; not intelligently and purposefully. You can see that if you are mentally antagonistic to any part, you cannot be in complete harmony with the Whole; therefore, as Jesus directed, be reconciled to everybody and everything before you offer worship.

Want for everybody all that you want for yourself.

The reader is recommended to read what we have said in a former work[1] concerning the Competitive mind and the Creative mind. It is very doubtful whether one who has lost health can completely regain it so long as he remains in the competitive mind.

Being on the Creative or Good-Will plane in mind, the next step is to form a conception of yourself as in perfect health, and to hold no thoughts which are not in full harmony with this conception. Have FAITH that if you think only thoughts of health you will establish in your physical body

1. The Science of Getting Rich.

the functioning of health; and use your will to determine that you will think only thoughts of health. Never think of yourself as sick, or as likely to be sick; never think of sickness in connection with yourself at all. And, as far as may be, shut out of your mind all thoughts of sickness in connection with others. Surround yourself as much as possible with the things which suggest the ideas of strength and health.

Have faith in health, and accept health as an actual present fact in your life. Claim health as a blessing bestowed upon you by the Supreme Life, and be deeply grateful at all times. Claim the blessing by faith; know that it is yours, and never admit a contrary thought to your mind.

Use your will-power to withhold your attention from every appearance of disease in yourself and others; do not study disease, think about it, nor speak of it. At all times, when the thought of disease is thrust upon you, move forward into the mental position of prayerful gratitude for your perfect health.

The mental actions necessary to being well may now be summed up in a single sentence: Form a conception of yourself in perfect health, and think only those thoughts which are in harmony with that conception.

That, with faith and gratitude, and the purpose to really live, covers all the requirements. It is not necessary to take mental exercises of any kind, except as described in Chapter VI, or to do wearying "stunts" in the way of affirmations, and so on. It is not necessary to concentrate the mind on the affected parts; it is far better not to think of any part as affected. It is not necessary to "treat" yourself by auto-suggestion, or to have others treat you in any way whatever.

The power that heals is the Principle of Health within you; and to call this Principle into Constructive Action it is only necessary, having harmonized yourself with the All-Mind, to claim by FAITH the All-Health; and to hold that claim until it is physically manifested in all the functions of your body.

In order to hold this mental attitude of faith, gratitude, and health, however, your external acts must be only those of health. You cannot long hold the internal attitude of a well person if you continue to perform the external acts of a sick person. It is essential not only that your every thought should be a thought of health, but that your every act should be an act of health, performed in a healthy manner. If you will make every thought a thought of health, and every conscious act an act of health, it must infallibly follow that every internal and unconscious function shall come to be healthy; for all the power of life is being continually exerted toward health. We shall next consider how you may make every act an act of health.

Chapter 9

When to Eat

You cannot build and maintain a perfectly healthy body by mental action alone, or by the performance of the unconscious or involuntary functions alone. There are certain actions, more or less voluntary, which have a direct and immediate relation with the continuance of life itself; these are eating, drinking, breathing, and sleeping. No matter what man's thought or mental attitude may be, he cannot live unless he eats, drinks, breathes, and sleeps; and, moreover, he cannot be well if he eats, drinks, breathes, and sleeps in an unnatural or wrong manner. It is therefore vitally important that you should learn the right way to perform these voluntary functions, and I shall proceed to show you this way, beginning with the matter of eating, which is most important.

There has been a vast amount of controversy as to when to eat, what to eat, how to eat, and how much to eat; and all this controversy is unnecessary, for the Right Way is very easy to find. You have only to consider the Law which governs all attainment, whether of health, wealth, power, or happiness; and that law is *that you must do what you can do now, where you are now; do every separate act in the most perfect manner possible, and put the power of faith into every action.*

The processes of digestion and assimilation are under the supervision and control of an inner division of man's mentality, which is generally called the sub-conscious mind; and I shall use that term here in order to be understood. The sub-conscious mind is in charge of all the functions and processes of life; and when more food is needed by the body, it makes the fact known by causing a sensation called hunger. Whenever food is needed, and can be used, there is hunger; and whenever there is hunger it is time to eat. When there is no hunger it is unnatural and wrong to eat, no matter how great may APPEAR to be the need for food. Even if you are in a condition of apparent starvation, with great emaciation, if there is no hunger you may know that FOOD CANNOT BE USED, and it will be unnatural and wrong for you to eat. Though you have not eaten for days, weeks, or months, if you have no hunger you may be perfectly sure that food cannot be used, and will probably not be used if taken. Whenever food is needed, if there is power to digest and assimilate it, so that it can be normally used, the sub-conscious mind will announce the fact by a decided hunger. Food, taken when there is no hunger, will sometimes be digested and assimilated, because Nature makes a special effort to perform the task which is thrust upon her against her will; but if food be habitually taken when there is no hunger, the digestive power is at last destroyed, and numberless evils caused.

If the foregoing be true—and it is indisputably so—it is a self-evident proposition that the natural time, and the healthy time, to eat is when one is hungry; and that it is never a natural or a healthy action to eat when one is not hungry. You see, then, that it is an easy matter to scientifically settle the question when to eat. ALWAYS eat when you are hungry; and NEVER eat when you are not hungry. This is obedience to nature, which is obedience to God.

We must not fail, however, to make clear the distinction between hunger and appetite. Hunger is the call of the sub-conscious mind for more material to be used in repairing and renewing the body, and in keeping up the internal heat; and hunger is never felt unless there is need for more material, and unless there is power to digest it when taken into the stomach. Appetite is a desire for the gratification of sensation. The drunkard has an appetite for liquor, but he cannot have a hunger for it. A normally fed person cannot have a hunger for candy or sweets; the desire for these things is an appetite. You cannot hunger for tea, coffee, spiced foods, or for the various taste-tempting devices of the skilled cook; if you desire these things, it is with appetite, not with hunger. Hunger is nature's call for material to be used in building new cells, and nature never calls for anything which may not be legitimately used for this purpose.

Appetite is often largely a matter of habit; if one eats or drinks at a certain hour, and especially if one takes sweetened or spiced and stimulating foods, the desire comes regularly at the same hour; but this habitual desire for food should never be mistaken for hunger. Hunger does not appear at specified times. It only comes when work or exercise has destroyed sufficient tissue to make the taking in of new raw material a necessity.

For instance, if a person has been sufficiently fed on the preceding day, it is impossible that he should feel a genuine hunger on arising from refreshing sleep. In sleep the body is recharged with vital power, and the assimilation of the food which has been taken during the day is completed; the system has no need for food immediately after sleep, unless the person went to his rest in a state of starvation. With a system of feeding, which is even a reasonable approach to a natural one, no one can have a real hunger for an early morning breakfast. There is no such thing possible as a normal or genuine hunger immediately after arising from sound sleep. The early morning breakfast is always taken to gratify appetite, never to satisfy hunger. No matter who you are, or what your condition is; no matter how hard you work, or how much you are exposed, unless you go to your bed starved, you cannot arise from your bed hungry.

Hunger is not caused by sleep, but by work. And it does not matter who you are, or what your condition, or how hard or easy your work, the so-called no-breakfast plan is the right plan for you. It is the right plan for everybody, because it is based on the universal law that hunger never comes until it is EARNED.

I am aware that a protest against this will come from the large number of people who "enjoy" their breakfasts; whose breakfast is their "best meal"; who believe that their work is so hard that they cannot "get through the forenoon on an empty stomach," and so on. But all their arguments fall down before the facts. They enjoy their breakfast as the toper enjoys his morning dram, because it gratifies a habitual appetite and not because it supplies a natural want. It is their best meal for the same reason that his morning dram is the toper's best drink. And they CAN get along without it, because millions of people, of every trade and profession, DO get along without it, and are vastly better for doing so. If you are to live according to the Science of Being Well, you must NEVER EAT UNTIL YOU HAVE AN EARNED HUNGER.

But if I do not eat on arising in the morning, when shall I take my first meal?

In ninety-nine cases out of a hundred twelve o'clock, noon, is early enough; and it is generally the most convenient time. If you are doing heavy work, you will get by noon a hunger sufficient to justify a good-sized meal; and if your work is light, you will probably still have hunger enough for a moderate meal. The best general rule or law that can be laid down is that you should eat your first meal of the day at noon, if you are hungry; and if you are not hungry, wait until you become so.

And when shall I eat my second meal?

Not at all, unless you are hungry for it; and that with a genuine earned hunger. If you do get hungry for a second meal, eat at the most convenient time; but do not eat until you have a really earned hunger. The reader who wishes to fully inform himself as to the reasons for this way of arranging the mealtimes will find the best books thereon cited in the preface to this work. From the foregoing, however, you can easily see that the Science of Being Well readily answers the question: When, and how often shall I eat? The answer is: Eat when you have an earned hunger; and never eat at any other time.

Chapter 10

What to Eat

The current sciences of medicine and hygiene have made no progress toward answering the question, What shall I eat? The contests between the vegetarians and the meat eaters, the cooked food advocates, raw food advocates, and various other "schools" of theorists, seem to be interminable; and from the mountains of evidence and argument piled up for and against each special theory, it is plain that if we depend on these scientists we shall never know what is the natural food of man. Turning away from the whole controversy, then, we will ask the question of nature herself, and we shall find that she has not left us without an answer.

Most of the errors of dietary scientists grow out of a false premise as to the natural state of man. It is assumed that civilization and mental development are unnatural things; that the man who lives in a modern house, in city or country, and who works in modern trade or industry for his living is leading an unnatural life, and is in an unnatural environment; that the only "natural" man is a naked savage, and that the farther we get from the savage the farther we are from nature. This is wrong. The man who has all that art and science can give him is leading the most natural life, because he is living most completely in all his faculties. The dweller in a well-appointed city flat, with modern conveniences and good ventilation, is living a far more naturally human life than the Australian savage who lives in a hollow tree or a hole in the ground.

That Great Intelligence, which is in all and through all, has in reality practically settled the question as to what we shall eat. In ordering the affairs of nature, It has decided that man's food shall be according to the zone in which he lives. In the frigid regions of the far North, fuel foods are required. The development of brain is not large, nor is the life severe in its labor-tax on muscle; and so the Esquimaux live largely on the blubber and fat of aquatic animals. No other diet is possible to them; they could not get fruits, nuts, or vegetables even if they were disposed to eat them; and they could not live on them in that climate if they could get them. So, notwithstanding the arguments of the vegetarians, the Esquimaux will continue to live on animal fats.

On the other hand, as we come toward the tropics, we find fuel foods less required; and we find the people naturally inclining toward a vegetarian diet. Millions live on rice and fruits; and the food regimen of an Esquimaux village, if followed upon the equator, would result in speedy death. A "natural" diet for the equatorial regions would be very far from being a natural diet near the North Pole; and the people of either zone, if not interfered with by medical or dietary "scientists," will be guided by the All Intelligence, which seeks the fullest life in all, to feed themselves in the best way for the promotion of perfect health. In general, you can see that God, working in nature and in the evolution of human society and customs, has answered your question as to what you shall eat; and I advise you to take His answer in preference to that of any man.

In the temperate zone the largest demands are made on man in spirit, mind, and body; and here we find the greatest variety of foods provided by nature. And it is really quite useless and superfluous to theorize on the question what the masses shall eat, for they have no choice; they must eat the foods which are staple products of the zone in which they live. It is impossible to supply all the people with a nut-and-fruit or raw food diet; and the fact that it is impossible is proof positive that these are not the foods intended by nature, for nature, being formed for the advancement of life, has not made the obtaining of the means of life an impossibility. So, I say, the question, What shall I eat? has been answered for you. Eat wheat, corn, rye, oats, barley, buckwheat; eat vegetables; eat meats, eat fruits, eat the things that are eaten by the masses of the people around the world, for in this matter the voice of the people is the voice of God. They have been led, generally, to the selection of certain foods; and they have been led, generally, to prepare these foods in generally similar ways; and you may depend upon it that in general they have the right foods and are preparing them in the right way. In these matters the race has been under the guidance of God. The list of foods in common use is a long one, and you must select there from according to your individual taste; if you do, you will find that you have an infallible guide, as shown in the next two chapters.

If you do not eat until you have an EARNED hunger, you will not find your taste demanding unnatural or unhealthy foods. The woodchopper, who has swung his axe continuously from seven in the morning until noon does not come in clamoring for cream puffs and confectionery; he wants pork and beans, or beefsteak and potatoes, or corn bread and cabbage; he asks for the plain solids. Offer to crack him a few walnuts and give him a plate of lettuce, and you will be met with huge disdain; those things are not natural foods for a workingman. And if they are not natural foods for a workingman, they are not for any other man; for work hunger is the only real hunger, and requires the same materials to satisfy it, whether it be in woodchopper or banker, in man, woman or child.

It is a mistake to suppose that food must be selected with anxious care to fit the vocation of the person who eats. It is not true that the woodchopper requires "heavy" or "solid" foods and the bookkeeper "light" foods. If you are a bookkeeper, or other brain worker, and do not eat until you have an EARNED hunger, you will want exactly the same foods that the woodchopper wants. Your body is made of exactly the same elements as that of the woodchopper, and requires the same materials for cell-building; why, then, feed him on ham and eggs and corn bread and you on crackers and toast? True, most of his waste is of muscle, while most of yours is of brain and nerve tissue; but it is also true that the woodchopper's diet contains all the requisites for brain and nerve building in far better proportions than they are found in most "light" foods. The world's best brain work has been done on the fare of the working people. The world's greatest thinkers have invariably lived on the plain solid foods common among the masses.

Let the bookkeeper wait until he has an earned hunger before he eats; and then, if he wants ham, eggs, and corn bread, by all means let him eat them; but let him remember that he does not need one-twentieth of the amount necessary for the woodchopper. It is not eating "hearty" foods which gives the brain worker indigestion; it is eating as much as would be needed by a muscle worker. Indigestion is never caused by eating to satisfy hunger; it is always caused by eating to gratify appetite. If you eat in the manner prescribed in the next chapter, your taste will soon become so natural that you will never WANT anything that you cannot eat with impunity; and you can drop the whole anxious question of what to eat from your mind forever, and simply eat what you want. Indeed, that is the only way to do if you are to think no thoughts but those of health; for you cannot think health so long as you are in continual doubt and uncertainty as to whether you are getting the right bills of fare.

"Take no thought what ye shall eat," said Jesus, and he spoke wisely. The foods found on the table of any ordinary middle-class or working class family will nourish your body perfectly if you eat at the right times and in the right way. If you want meat, eat it; and if you do not want it, do not eat it, and do not suppose that you must find some special substitute for it. You can live perfectly well on what is left on any table after the meat has been removed.

It is not necessary to worry about a "varied" diet, so as to get in all the necessary elements. The Chinese and Hindus build very good bodies and excellent brains on a diet of few variations, rice making almost the whole of it. The Scotch are physically and mentally strong on oatmeal cakes; and the Irishman is husky of body and brilliant of mind on potatoes and pork. The wheat berry contains practically all that is necessary for the building of brain and body; and a man can live very well on a monodiet of navy beans.

Form a conception of perfect health for yourself, and do not hold any thought which is not a thought of health.

NEVER eat until you have an EARNED HUNGER. Remember that it will not hurt you in the least to go hungry for a short time; but it will surely hurt you to eat when you are not hungry.

Do not give the least thought to what you should or should not eat; simply eat what is set before you, selecting that which pleases your taste most. In other words, eat what you want. This you can do with perfect results if you eat in the right way; and how to do this will be explained in the next chapter.

Chapter 11

How to Eat

It is a settled fact that man naturally chews his food. The few faddists who maintain that we should bolt our nourishment, after the manner of the dog and others of the lower animals, can no longer get a hearing; we know that we should chew our food. And if it is natural that we should chew our food, the more thoroughly we chew it the more completely natural the process must be. If you will chew every mouthful to a liquid, you need not be in the least concerned as to what you shall eat, for you can get sufficient nourishment out of any ordinary food.

Whether or not this chewing shall be an irksome and laborious task or a most enjoyable process, depends upon the mental attitude in which you come to the table.

If your mind and attitude are on other things, or if you are anxious or worried about business or domestic affairs, you will find it almost impossible to eat without bolting more or less of your food. You must learn to live so scientifically that you will have no business or domestic cares to worry about; this you can do, and you can also learn to give your undivided attention to the act of eating while at the table.

When you eat, do so with an eye single to the purpose of getting all the enjoyment you can from that meal; dismiss everything else from your mind, and do not let anything take your attention from the food and its taste until your meal is finished. Be cheerfully confident, for if you follow these instructions you may KNOW that the food you eat is exactly the right food, and that it will "agree" with you to perfection.

Sit down to the table with confident cheerfulness, and take a moderate portion of the food; take whatever thing looks most desirable to you. Do not select some food because you think it will be good for you; select that which will taste good to you. If you are to get well and stay well, you must drop the idea of doing things because they are good for your health, and do things because you want to do them. Select the food you want most; gratefully give thanks to God that you have learned how to eat it in such a way that digestion shall be perfect; and take a moderate mouthful of it.

Do not fix your attention on the act of chewing; fix it on the TASTE of the food; and taste and enjoy it until it is reduced to a liquid state and passes down your throat by involuntary swallowing. No matter how long it takes, do not think of the time. Think of the taste. Do not allow your eyes to wander over the table, speculating as to what you shall eat next; do not worry for fear there is not enough, and that you will not get your share of everything. Do not anticipate the taste of the next thing; keep your mind centered on the taste of what you have in your mouth. And that is all of it.

Scientific and healthful eating is a delightful process after you have learned how to do it, and after you have overcome the bad old habit of gobbling down your food unchewed. It is best not to have too much conversation going on while eating; be cheerful, but not talkative; do the talking afterward.

In most cases, some use of the will is required to form the habit of correct eating. The bolting habit is an unnatural one, and is without doubt mostly the result of fear. Fear that we will be robbed of our food; fear that we will not get our share of the good things; fear that we will lose precious time—these are the causes of haste. Then there is anticipation of the dainties that are to come for dessert, and the consequent desire to get at them as quickly as possible; and there is mental abstraction, or thinking of other matters while eating. All these must be overcome.

When you find that your mind is wandering, call a halt; think for a moment of the food, and of how good it tastes; of the perfect digestion and assimilation that are going to follow the meal, and begin again. Begin again and again, though you must do so twenty times in the course of a single meal; and again and again, though you must do so every meal for weeks and months. It is perfectly certain that you CAN form the "Fletcher habit" if you persevere; and when you have formed it, you will experience a healthful pleasure you have never known.

This is a vital point, and I must not leave it until I have thoroughly impressed it upon your mind. Given the right materials, perfectly prepared, the Principle of Health will positively build you a perfectly healthy body; and you cannot prepare the materials *perfectly* in any other way that the one I am describing. If you are to have perfect health, you MUST eat in just this way; you can, and the doing of it is only a matter of a little perseverance. What use for you to talk of mental control unless you will govern yourself in so simple a matter as ceasing to bolt your food? What use to talk of concentration unless you can keep your mind on the act of eating for so short a space as fifteen or twenty minutes, especially with all the pleasures of taste to help you? Go on, and conquer. In a few weeks, or months, as the case may be, you will find the habit of scientific eating becoming fixed; and soon you will be in so splendid a condition, mentally and physically, that nothing would induce you to return to the bad old way.

We have seen that if man will think only thoughts of perfect health, his internal functions will be performed in a healthy manner; and we have seen that in order to think thoughts of health, man must perform the voluntary functions in a healthy manner. The most important of the voluntary functions is that of eating; and we see, so far, no especial difficulty in eating in a perfectly healthy way. I will here summarize the instructions as to when to eat, what to eat, and how to eat, with the reasons therefore:—

NEVER eat until you have an EARNED hunger, no matter how long you go without food. This is based on the fact that whenever food is needed in the system, if there is power to digest it, the sub-conscious mind announces the need by the sensation of hunger. Learn to distinguish between genuine hunger and the gnawing and craving sensations caused by unnatural appetite. Hunger is never a disagreeable feeling, accompanied by weakness, faintness, or gnawing feelings at the stomach; it is a pleasant, anticipatory desire for food, and is felt mostly in the mouth and throat. It does not come at certain hours or at stated intervals; it only comes when the sub-conscious mind is ready to receive, digest, and assimilate food.

Eat whatever foods you want, making your selection from the staples in general use in the zone in which you live. The Supreme Intelligence has guided man to the selection of these foods, and they are the right ones for all. I am referring, of course, to the foods which are taken to satisfy hunger, not to those which have been contrived merely to gratify appetite or perverted taste. The instinct which has guided the masses of men to make use of the great staples of food to satisfy their hunger is a divine one. God has made no mistake; if you eat these foods you will not go wrong.

Eat your food with cheerful confidence, and get all the pleasure that is to be had from the taste of every mouthful. Chew each morsel to a liquid, keeping your attention fixed on the enjoyment of the process. This is the only way to eat in a perfectly complete and successful manner; and when anything is done in a completely successful manner, the general result cannot be a failure. In the attainment of health, the law is the same as in the attainment of riches; if you make each act a success in itself, the sum of all your acts must be a success.

When you eat in the mental attitude I have described, and in the manner I have described, nothing can be added to the process; it is done in a perfect manner, and it is successfully done. And if eating is successfully done, digestion, assimilation, and the building of a healthy body are successfully begun. We next take up the question of the quantity of food required.

Chapter 12

Hunger and Appetites

It is very easy to find the correct answer to the question, How much shall I eat? You are never to eat until you have an earned hunger, and you are to stop eating the instant you BEGIN to feel that your hunger is abating. Never gorge yourself; never eat to repletion. When you *begin* to feel that your hunger is satisfied, know that you have enough; for until you have enough, you will continue to feel the sensation of hunger. If you eat as directed in the last chapter, it is probable that you will begin to feel satisfied before you have taken half your usual amount; but stop there, all the same. No matter how delightfully attractive the dessert, or how tempting the pie or pudding, do not eat a mouthful of it if you find that your hunger has been in the least degree assuaged by the other foods you have taken.

Whatever you eat after your hunger begins to abate is taken to gratify taste and appetite, not hunger and is not called for by nature at all. It is therefore excess; mere debauchery, and it cannot fail to work mischief.

This is a point you will need to watch with nice discrimination, for the habit of eating purely for sensual gratification is very deeply rooted with most of us. The usual "dessert" of sweet and tempting foods is prepared solely with a view to inducing people to eat after hunger has been satisfied; and all the effects are evil. It is not that pie and cake are unwholesome foods; they are usually perfectly wholesome if eaten to satisfy hunger, and NOT to gratify appetite. If you want pie, cake, pastry or puddings, it is better to begin your meal with them, finishing with the plainer and less tasty foods. You will find, however, that if you eat as directed in the preceding chapters, the plainest food will soon come to taste like kingly fare to you; for your sense of taste, like all your other senses, will become so acute with the general improvement in your condition that you will find new delights in common things. No glutton ever enjoyed a meal like the man who eats for hunger only, who gets the most out of every mouthful, and who stops on the instant that he feels the edge taken from his hunger. The first intimation that hunger is abating is the signal from the sub-conscious mind that it is time to quit.

The average person who takes up this plan of living will be greatly surprised to learn how little food is really required to keep the body in perfect condition. The amount depends upon the work; upon how much muscular exercise is taken, and upon the extent to which the person is exposed to cold. The woodchopper who goes into the forest in the winter time and swings his axe all day can eat two full meals; but the brain worker who sits all day on a chair, in a warm room, does not need one third and often not one tenth as much. Most wood-choppers eat two or three times as much, and most brain workers from three to ten times as much as nature calls for; and the elimination of this vast amount of surplus rubbish from their systems is a tax on vital power which in time depletes their energy and leaves them an easy prey to so-called disease. Get all possible enjoyment out of the taste of your food, but never eat anything merely because it tastes good; and on the instant that you feel that your hunger is less keen, stop eating.

If you will consider for a moment, you will see that there is positively no other way for you to settle these various food questions than by adopting the plan here laid down for you. As to the proper time to eat, there is no other way to decide than to say that you should eat whenever you have an EARNED HUNGER. It is a self-evident proposition that that is the right time to eat, and that any other is a wrong time to eat. As to what to eat, the Eternal Wisdom has decided that the masses of men shall eat the staple products of the zones in which they live. The staple foods of your particular zone are the right foods for you; and the Eternal Wisdom, working in and through the minds of the masses of men, has taught them how best to prepare these foods by cooking and otherwise. And as to how to eat, you know that you must chew your food; and if it must be chewed, then reason tells us that the more thorough and perfect the operation the better.

I repeat that success in anything is attained by making each separate act a success in itself. If you make each action, however small and unimportant, a thoroughly successful action, your day's work as a whole cannot result in failure. If you make the actions of each day successful, the sum total of your life cannot be failure. A great success is the result of doing a large number of little things, and doing each one in a perfectly successful way. If every thought is a healthy thought, and if every action of your life is performed in a healthy way, you must soon attain to perfect health. It is impossible to devise a way in which you can perform the act of eating more successfully, and in a manner more in accord with the laws of life, than by chewing every mouthful to a liquid, enjoying the taste fully, and keeping a cheerful confidence the while. Nothing can be added to make the process more successful; while if anything be subtracted, the process will not be a completely healthy one.

In the matter of how much to eat, you will also see that there could be no other guide so natural, so safe, and so reliable as the one I have prescribed—to stop eating on the instant you feel that your hunger begins to abate. The sub-conscious mind may be trusted with implicit reliance to inform us when food is needed; and it may be trusted as implicitly to inform us when the need has been supplied. If ALL food is eaten for hunger, and NO food is taken merely to gratify taste, you will never eat too much; and if you eat whenever you have an EARNED hunger, you will always eat enough. By reading carefully the summing up in the following chapter, you will see that the requirements for eating in a perfectly healthy way are really very few and simple.

The matter of drinking in a natural way may be dismissed here with a very few words. If you wish to be exactly and rigidly scientific, drink nothing but water; drink only when you are thirsty; drink whenever you are thirsty, and stop as soon as you feel that your thirst begins to abate. But if you are living rightly in regard to eating, it will not be necessary to practice asceticism or great self-denial in the matter of drinking. You can take an occasional cup of weak coffee without harm; you can, to a reasonable extent, follow the customs of those around you. Do not get the soda fountain habit; do not drink merely to tickle your palate with sweet liquids; be sure that you take a drink of water whenever you feel thirst. Never be too lazy, too indifferent, or too busy to get a drink of water when you feel the least thirst; if you obey this rule, you will have little inclination to take strange and unnatural drinks. Drink only to satisfy thirst; drink whenever you feel thirst; and stop drinking as soon as you feel thirst abating. That is the perfectly healthy way to supply the body with the necessary fluid material for its internal processes.

Chapter 13

In a Nutshell

There is a Cosmic Life which permeates, penetrates, and fills the interspaces of the universe, being in and through all things. This Life is not merely a vibration, or form of energy; it is a Living Substance. All things are made from it; it is All, and in all.

This Substance thinks, and it assumes the form of that which it thinks about. The thought of a form, in this substance, creates the form; the thought of a motion institutes the motion. The visible universe, with all its forms and motions, exists because it is in the thought of Original Substance.

Man is a form of Original Substance, and can think original thoughts; and within himself, man's thoughts have controlling or formative power. The thought of a condition produces that condition; the thought of a motion institutes that motion. So long as man thinks of the conditions and motions of disease, so long will the conditions and motions of disease exist within him. If man will think only of perfect health, the Principle of Health within him will maintain normal conditions.

To be well, man must form a conception of perfect health, and hold thoughts harmonious with that conception as regards himself and all things. He must think only of healthy conditions and functioning; he must not permit a thought of unhealthy or abnormal conditions or functioning to find lodgment in his mind at any time.

In order to think only of healthy conditions and functioning, man must perform the voluntary acts of life in a perfectly healthy way. He cannot think perfect health so long as he knows that he is living in a wrong or unhealthy way; or even so long as he has doubts as to whether or not he is living in a healthy way. Man cannot think thoughts of perfect health while his voluntary functions are performed in the manner of one who is sick. The voluntary functions of life are eating, drinking, breathing, and sleeping. When man thinks only of healthy conditions and functioning, and performs these externals in a perfectly healthy manner, he must have perfect health.

In eating, man must learn to be guided by his hunger. He must distinguish between hunger and appetite, and between hunger and the cravings of habit; he must NEVER eat unless he feels an EARNED HUNGER. He must learn that genuine hunger is never present after natural sleep, and that the demand for an early morning meal is purely a matter of habit and appetite; and he must not begin his day by eating in violation of natural law. He must wait until he has an Earned Hunger, which, in most cases, will make his first meal come at about the noon hour. No matter what his condition, vocation, or circumstances, he must make it his rule not to eat until he has an EARNED HUNGER; and he may remember that it is far better to fast for several hours after he has become hungry than to eat before he begins to feel hunger. It will not hurt you to go hungry for a few hours, even though you are working hard; but it will hurt you to fill your stomach when you are not hungry, whether you are working or not. If you never eat until you have an Earned Hunger, you may be certain that in so far as the time of eating is concerned, you are proceeding in a perfectly healthy way. This is a self-evident proposition.

As to what he shall eat, man must be guided by that Intelligence which has arranged that the people of any given portion of the earth's surface must live on the staple products of the zone which they inhabit. Have faith in God, and ignore "food science" of every kind. Do not pay the slightest attention to the controversies as to the relative merits of cooked and raw foods; of vegetables and meats; or as to your need for carbohydrates and proteins. Eat only when you have an earned hunger, and then take the common foods of the masses of the people in the zone in which you live, and have perfect confidence that the results will be good. They will be. Do not seek for luxuries, or for things imported or fixed up to tempt the taste; stick to the plain solids; and when these do not "taste good," fast until they do. Do not seek for "light" foods; for easily digestible, or "healthy" foods; eat what the farmers and workingmen eat. Then you will be functioning in a perfectly healthy manner, so far as what to eat is concerned. I repeat, if you have no hunger or taste for the plain foods, do not eat at all; wait until hunger comes. Go without eating until the plainest food tastes good to you; and then begin your meal with what you like best.

In deciding how to eat, man must be guided by reason. We can see that the abnormal states of hurry and worry produced by wrong thinking about business and similar things have led us to form the habit of eating too fast, and chewing too little. Reason tells us that food should be chewed, and that the more thoroughly it is chewed the better it is prepared for the chemistry of digestion. Furthermore, we can see that the man who eats slowly and chews his food to a liquid, keeping his mind on the process and giving it his undivided attention, will enjoy more of the pleasure of taste than he who bolts his food with his mind on something else. To eat in a perfectly healthy manner, man must concentrate his attention on the act, with cheerful enjoyment and confidence; he must taste his food, and he must reduce each mouthful to a liquid before swallowing it. The foregoing instructions, if followed, make the function of eating completely perfect; nothing can be added as to what, when, and how.

In the matter of how much to eat, man must be guided by the same inward intelligence, or Principle of Health, which tells him when food is wanted. He must stop eating in the moment that he feels hunger abating; he must not eat beyond this point to gratify taste. If he ceases to eat in the instant that the inward demand for food ceases, he will never overeat; and the function of supplying the body with food will be performed in a perfectly healthy manner.

The matter of eating naturally is a very simple one; there is nothing in all the foregoing that cannot be easily practiced by any one. This method, put in practice, will infallibly result in perfect digestion and assimilation; and all anxiety and careful thought concerning the matter can at once be dropped from the mind. Whenever you have an earned hunger, eat with thankfulness what is set before you, chewing each mouthful to a liquid, and stopping when you feel the edge taken from your hunger.

The importance of the mental attitude is sufficient to justify an additional word. While you are eating, as at all other times, think only of healthy conditions and normal functioning. Enjoy what you eat; if you carry on a conversation at the table, talk of the goodness of the food, and of the pleasure it is giving you. Never mention that you dislike this or that; speak only of those things which you like. Never discuss the wholesomeness or unwholesomeness of foods; never mention or think of unwholesomeness at all. If there is anything on the table for which you do not care, pass it by in silence, or with a word of commendation; never criticise or object to anything. Eat your food with gladness and with singleness of heart, praising God and giving thanks. Let your watchword be perseverance; whenever you fall into the old way of hasty eating, or of wrong thought and speech, bring yourself up short and begin again.

It is of the most vital importance to you that you should be a self-controlling and self-directing person; and you can never hope to become so unless you can master yourself in so simple and fundamental a matter as the manner and method of your eating. If you cannot control yourself in this, you cannot control yourself in anything that will be worthwhile. On the other hand, if you carry out the foregoing instructions, you may rest in the assurance that in so far as right thinking and right eating are concerned you are living in a perfectly scientific way; and you may also be assured that if you practice what is prescribed in the following chapters you will quickly build your body into a condition of perfect health.

Chapter 14

Breathing

The function of breathing is a vital one, and it immediately concerns the continuance of life. We can live many hours without sleeping, and many days without eating or drinking, but only a few minutes without breathing. The act of breathing is involuntary, but the manner of it, and the provision of the proper conditions for its healthy performance, falls within the scope of volition. Man will continue to breathe involuntarily, but he can voluntarily determine what he shall breathe, and how deeply and thoroughly he shall breathe; and he can, of his own volition, keep the physical mechanism in condition for the perfect performance of the function.

It is essential, if you wish to breathe in a perfectly healthy way, that the physical machinery used in the act should be kept in good condition. You must keep your spine moderately straight, and the muscles of your chest must be flexible and free in action. You cannot breathe in the right way if your shoulders are greatly stooped forward and your chest hollow and rigid. Sitting or standing at work in a slightly stooping position tends to produce hollow chest; so does lifting heavy weights—or light weights.

The tendency of work, of almost all kinds, is to pull the shoulders forward, curve the spine, and flatten the chest; and if the chest is greatly flattened, full and deep breathing becomes impossible, and perfect health is out of the question.

Various gymnastic exercises have been devised to counteract the effect of stooping while at work; such as hanging by the hands from a swing or trapeze bar, or sitting on a chair with the feet under some heavy article of furniture and bending backward until the head touches the floor, and so on. All these are good enough in their way, but very few people will follow them long enough and regularly enough to accomplish any real gain in physique. The taking of "health exercises" of any kind is burdensome and unnecessary; there is a more natural, simpler, and much better way.

This better way is to keep yourself straight, and to breathe deeply. Let your mental conception of yourself be that you are a perfectly straight person, and whenever the matter comes to your mind, be sure that you instantly expand your chest, throw back your shoulders, and "straighten up." Whenever you do this, slowly draw in your breath until you fill your lungs to their utmost capacity; "crowd in" all the air you possibly can; and while holding it for an instant in the lungs, throw your shoulders still further back, and stretch your chest;

at the same time try to pull your spine forward between the shoulders. Then let the air go easily.

This is the one great exercise for keeping the chest full, flexible, and in good condition. Straighten up; fill your lungs FULL; stretch your chest and straighten your spine, and exhale easily. And this exercise you must repeat, in season and out of season, at all times and in all places, until you form a habit of doing it; you can easily do so. Whenever you step out of doors into the fresh, pure air, BREATHE. When you are at work, and think of yourself and your position, BREATHE. When you are in company, and are reminded of the matter, BREATHE. When you are awake in the night, BREATHE. No matter where you are or what you are doing, whenever the idea comes to your mind, straighten up and BREATHE. If you walk to and from your work, take the exercise all the way; it will soon become a delight to you; you will keep it up, not for the sake of health, but as a matter of pleasure.

Do not consider this a "health exercise"; *never take health exercises, or do gymnastics to make you well. To do so is to recognize sickness as a present fact or as a possibility, which is precisely what you must not do.* The people who are always taking exercises for their health are always thinking about being sick. It ought to be a matter of pride with you to keep your spine straight and strong; as much so as it is to keep your face clean. Keep your spine straight, and your chest full and flexible for the same reason that you keep your hands clean and your nails manicured; because it is slovenly to do otherwise. Do it without a thought of sickness, present or possible. You must either be crooked and unsightly, or you must be straight; and if you are straight your breathing will take care of itself. You will find the matter of health exercises referred to again in a future chapter.

It is essential, however, that you should breathe AIR. It appears to be the intention of nature that the lungs should receive air containing its regular percentage of oxygen, and not greatly contaminated by other gases, or by filth of any kind. Do not allow yourself to think that you are compelled to live or work where the air is not fit to breathe. If your house cannot be properly ventilated, move; and if you are employed where the air is bad, get another job; you can, by practicing the methods given in the preceding volume of this series—"THE SCIENCE OF GETTING RICH." If no one would consent to work in bad air, employers would speedily see to it that all work rooms were properly ventilated. The worst air is that from which the oxygen has been exhausted by breathing; as that of churches and theaters where crowds of people congregate, and the outlet and supply of air are poor. Next to this is air containing other gases than oxygen and hydrogen—sewer gas, and the effluvium from decaying things. Air that is heavily charged with dust or particles of organic matter may be endured better than any of these. Small particles of organic matter other than food are generally thrown off from the lungs; but gases go into the blood.

I speak advisedly when I say "other than food." Air is largely a food. It is the most thoroughly alive thing we take into the body. Every breath carries in millions of microbes, many of which are assimilated. The odors from earth, grass, tree, flower, plant, and from cooking foods are foods in themselves; they are minute particles of the substances from which they come, and are often so attenuated that they pass directly from the lungs into the blood, and are assimilated without digestion. And the atmosphere is permeated with the One Original Substance, which is life itself. Consciously recognize this whenever you think of your breathing, and think that you are breathing in life; you really are, and conscious recognition helps the process. See to it that you do not breathe air containing poisonous gases, and that you do not re-breathe the air which has been used by yourself or others.

That is all there is to the matter of breathing correctly. Keep your spine straight and your chest flexible, and breathe pure air, recognizing with thankfulness the fact that you breathe in the Eternal Life. That is not difficult; and beyond these things give little thought to your breathing except to thank God that you have learned how to do it perfectly.

Chapter 15

Sleep

Vital power is renewed in sleep. Every living thing sleeps; men, animals, reptiles, fish, and insects sleep, and even plants have regular periods of slumber. And this is because it is in sleep that we come into such contact with the Principle of Life in nature that our own lives may be renewed. It is in sleep that the brain of man is recharged with vital energy, and the Principle of Health within him is given new strength. It is of the first importance, then, that we should sleep in a natural, normal, and perfectly healthy manner.

Studying sleep, we note that the breathing is much deeper, and more forcible and rhythmic than in the waking state. Much more air is inspired when asleep than when awake, and this tells us that the Principle of Health requires large quantities of some element in the atmosphere for the process of renewal. If you would surround sleep with natural conditions, then, the first step is to see that you have an unlimited supply of fresh and pure air to breathe. Physicians have found that sleeping in the pure air of out-of-doors is very efficacious in the treatment of pulmonary troubles; and, taken in connection with the Way of Living and Thinking prescribed in this book, you will find that it is just as efficacious in curing every other sort of trouble. Do not take any half-way measures in this matter of securing pure air while you sleep. Ventilate your bedroom thoroughly; so thoroughly that it will be practically the same as sleeping out of doors. Have a door or window open wide; have one open on each side of the room, if possible. If you cannot have a good draught of air across the room, pull the head of your bed close to the open window, so that the air from without may come fully into your face. No matter how cold or unpleasant the weather, have a window open, and open wide; and try to get a circulation of pure air through the room. Pile on the bedclothes, if necessary, to keep you warm; but have an unlimited supply of fresh air from out of doors. This is the first great requisite for healthy sleep.

The brain and nerve centers cannot be thoroughly vitalized if you sleep in "dead" or stagnant air; you must have the living atmosphere, vital with nature's Principle of Life. I repeat, do not make any compromise in this matter; ventilate your sleeping room completely, and see that there is a circulation of outdoor air through it while you sleep. You are not sleeping in a perfectly healthy way if you shut the doors and windows of your sleeping room, whether in winter or summer. Have fresh air. If you are where there is no fresh air, move. If your bedroom cannot be ventilated, get into another house.

Next in importance is the mental attitude in which you go to sleep. It is well to sleep intelligently, purposefully, knowing what you do it for. Lie down thinking that sleep is an infallible vitalizer, and go to sleep with a confident faith that your strength is to be renewed; that you will awake full of vitality and health. Put purpose into your sleep as you do into your eating; give the matter your attention for a few minutes, as you go to rest. Do not seek your couch with a discouraged or depressed feeling; go there joyously, to be made whole. Do not forget the exercise of gratitude in going to sleep; before you close your eyes, give thanks to God for having shown you the way to perfect health, and go to sleep with this grateful thought uppermost in your mind. A bedtime prayer of thanksgiving is a mighty good thing; it puts the Principle of Health within you into communication with its source, from which it is to receive new power while you are in the silence of unconsciousness.

You may see that the requirements for perfectly healthy sleep are not difficult. First, to see that you breathe pure air from out of doors while you sleep; and, second, to put the Within into touch with the Living Substance by a few minutes of grateful meditation as you go to bed. Observe these requirements, go to sleep in a thankful and confident frame of mind, and all will be well. If you have insomnia, do not let it worry you. While you lie awake, form your conception of health; meditate with thankfulness on the abundant life which is yours, breathe, and feel perfectly confident that you will sleep in due time; and you will. Insomnia, like every other ailment, must give way before the Principle of Health aroused to full constructive activity by the course of thought and action herein described.

The reader will now comprehend that it is not at all burdensome or disagreeable to perform the voluntary functions of life in a perfectly healthy way. The perfectly healthy way is the easiest, simplest, most natural, and most pleasant way. The cultivation of health is not a work of art, difficulty, or strenuous labor. You have only to lay aside artificial observances of every kind, and eat, drink, breathe, and sleep in the most natural and delightful way; and if you do this, thinking health and only health, you will certainly be well.

Chapter 16

Supplementary Instructions

In forming a conception of health, it is necessary to think of the manner in which you would live and work if you were perfectly well and very strong; to imagine yourself doing things in the way of a perfectly well and very strong person, until you have a fairly good conception of what you would be if you were well. Then take a mental and physical attitude in harmony with this conception; and do not depart from this attitude. You must unify yourself in thought with the thing you desire; and whatever state or condition you unify with yourself in thought will soon become unified with you in body. The scientific way is to sever relations with everything you do not want, and to enter into relations with everything you do want. Form a conception of perfect health, and relate yourself to this conception in word, act, and attitude.

Guard your speech; make every word harmonize with the conception of perfect health. Never complain; never say things like these: "I did not sleep well last night;" "I have a pain in my side;" "I do not feel at all well to-day," and so on. Say "I am looking forward to a good night's sleep to-night;" "I can see that I progress rapidly," and things of similar meaning. In so far as everything which is connected with disease is concerned, your way is to forget it; and in so far as everything which is connected with health is concerned, your way is to unify yourself with it in thought and speech.

This is the whole thing in a nutshell: *make yourself one with Health in thought, word, and action; and do not connect yourself with sickness either by thought, word, or action.*

Do not read "Doctor Books" or medical literature, or the literature of those whose theories conflict with those herein set forth; to do so will certainly undermine your faith in the Way of Living upon which you have entered, and cause you to again come into mental relations with disease. This book really gives you all that is required; nothing essential has been omitted, and practically all the superfluous has been eliminated. The Science of Being Well is an exact science, like arithmetic; nothing can be added to the fundamental principles, and if anything be taken from them, a failure will result. If you follow strictly the way of living prescribed in this book, you will be well; and you certainly CAN follow this way, both in thought and action.

Relate not only yourself, but so far as possible all others, in your thoughts, to perfect health. Do not sympathize with people when they complain, or even when they are sick and suffering. Turn their thoughts into a constructive channel if you can; do all you can for their relief, but do it with the health thought in your mind. Do not let people tell their woes and catalogue their symptoms to you; turn the conversation to some other subject, or excuse yourself and go. Better be considered an unfeeling person than to have the disease thought forced upon you. When you are in company of people whose conversational stock-in-trade is sickness and kindred matters, ignore what they say and fall to offering a mental prayer of gratitude for your perfect health; and if that does not enable you to shut out their thoughts, say good-by and leave them. No matter what they think or say; politeness does not require you to permit yourself to be poisoned by diseased or perverted thought. When we have a few more hundreds of thousands of enlightened thinkers who will not stay where people complain and talk sickness, the world will advance rapidly toward health. When you let people talk to you of sickness, you assist them to increase and multiply sickness.

What shall I do when I am in pain? Can one be in actual physical suffering and still think only thoughts of *health*?

Yes. Do not resist pain; recognize that it is a good thing. Pain is caused by an effort of the Principle of Health to overcome some unnatural condition; this you must know and feel. When you have a pain, think that a process of healing is going on in the affected part, and mentally assist and co-operate with it. Put yourself in full mental harmony with the power which is causing the pain; assist it; help it along. Do not hesitate, when necessary, to use hot fomentations and similar means to further the good work which is going on. If the pain is severe, lie down and give your mind to the work of quietly and easily co-operating with the force which is at work for your good. This is the time to exercise gratitude and faith; be thankful for the power of health which is causing the pain, and be certain that the pain will cease as soon as the good work is done. Fix your thoughts, with confidence, on the Principle of Health which is making such conditions within you that pain will soon be unnecessary. You will be surprised to find how easily you can conquer pain; and after you have lived for a time in this Scientific Way, pains and aches will be things unknown to you.

What shall I do when I am too weak for my work? Shall I drive myself beyond my strength, trusting in God to support me? Shall I go on, like the runner, expecting a "second wind"?

No; better not. When you begin to live in this Way, you will probably not be of normal strength; and you will gradually pass from a low physical condition to a higher one. If you relate yourself mentally with health and strength, and perform the voluntary functions of life in a perfectly healthy manner, your strength will increase from day to day; but for a time you may have days when your strength is insufficient for the work you would like to do. At such times rest, and exercise gratitude. Recognize the fact that your strength is growing rapidly, and feel a deep thankfulness to the Living One from whom it comes. Spend an hour of weakness in thanksgiving and rest, with full faith that great strength is at hand; and then get up and go on again. While you rest do not think of your present weakness; *think of the strength that is coming.*

Never, at any time, allow yourself to think that you are giving way to weakness; when you rest, as when you go to sleep, fix your mind on the Principle of Health which is building you into complete strength.

What shall I do about that great bugaboo which scares millions of people to death every year—Constipation?

Do nothing. Read Horace Fletcher on "The A B Z or Our Own Nutrition," and get the full force of his explanation of the fact that when you live on this scientific plan you need not, and indeed cannot, have an evacuation of the bowels every day; and that an operation in from once in three days to once in two weeks is quite sufficient for perfect health. The gross feeders who eat from three to ten times as much as can be utilized in their systems have a great amount of waste to eliminate; but if you live in the manner we have described it will be otherwise with you.

If you eat only when you have an EARNED HUNGER, and chew every mouthful to a liquid, and if you stop eating the instant you BEGIN to be conscious of an abatement of your hunger, you will so perfectly prepare your food for digestion and assimilation that practically all of it will be taken up by the absorbents; and there will be little—almost nothing—remaining in the bowels to be excreted. If you are able to entirely banish from your memory all that you have read in "doctor books" and patent medicine advertisements concerning constipation, you need give the matter no further thought at all. The Principle of Health will take care of it.

But if your mind has been filled with fear-thought in regard to constipation, it may be well in the beginning for you to occasionally flush the colon with warm water. There is not the least need of doing it, except to make the process of your mental emancipation from fear a little easier; it may be worthwhile for that. And as soon as you see that you are making good progress, and that you have cut down your quantity of food, and are really eating in the Scientific Way, dismiss constipation from your mind forever; you have nothing more to do with it. Put your trust in that Principle within you which has the power to give you perfect health; relate It by your reverent gratitude to the Principle of Life which is All Power, and go on your way rejoicing.

What about exercise?

Every one is the better for a little all-round use of the muscles every day; and the best way to get this is to do it by engaging in some form of play or amusement. Get your exercise in the natural way; as recreation, not as a forced stunt for health's sake alone. Ride a horse or a bicycle; play tennis or tenpins, or toss a ball. Have some avocation like gardening in which you can spend an hour every day with pleasure and profit; there are a thousand ways in which you can get exercise enough to keep your body supple and your circulation good, and yet not fall into the rut of "exercising for your health." Exercise for fun or profit; exercise because you are too healthy to sit still, and not because you wish to become healthy, or to remain so.

Are long continued fasts necessary?

Seldom, if ever. The Principle of Health does not often require twenty, thirty, or forty days to get ready for action; under normal conditions, hunger will come in much less time. In most long fasts, the reason hunger does not come sooner is because it has been inhibited by the patient himself. He begins the fast with the FEAR if not actually with the hope that it will be many days before hunger comes; the literature he has read on the subject has prepared him to expect a long fast, and he is grimly determined to go to a finish, let the time be as long as it will. And the sub-conscious mind, under the influence of powerful and positive suggestion, suspends hunger.

When, for any reason, nature takes away your hunger, go cheerfully on with your usual work, and do not eat until she gives it back. No matter if it is two, three, ten days, or longer; you may be perfectly sure that when it is time for you to eat you will be hungry; and if you are cheerfully confident and keep your faith in health, you will suffer from no weakness or discomfort caused by abstinence. When you are not hungry, you will feel stronger, happier, and more comfortable if you do not eat than you will if you do eat; no matter how long the fast. And if you live in the scientific way described in this book, you will never have to take long fasts; you will seldom miss a meal, and you will enjoy your meals more than ever before in your life. Get an earned hunger before you eat; and whenever you get an earned hunger, eat.

INTERNATIONAL BESTSELLER

THE POWER OF YOUR SUBCONSCIOUS MIND

by Dr. Joseph Murphy

Pages : 232
Size : 8 x 5.25 inches
Binding : Paperback
Language : English
Subject : Self-Help
ISBN : 9788180320958

'The Power of Your Subconscious Mind' has been a bestseller since its first publication in 1963, selling many millions of copies since its original publication. It is one of the most brilliant and beloved spiritual self-help works of all time which can help you heal yourself, banish your fears, sleep better, enjoy better relationships and just feel happier. The techniques are simple and results come quickly. You can improve your relationships, your finances, your physical well-being.

Dr Joseph Murphy explains that life events are actually the result of the workings of your conscious and subconscious minds. He suggests practical techniques through which one can change one's destiny, principally by focusing and redirecting this miraculous energy. Years of research studying the world's major religions convinced him that some Great Power lay behind all spiritual life and that this power is within each of us.

'The Power of Your Subconscious Mind' will open a world of success, happiness, prosperity, and peace for you.

OTHER BOOKS YOU MAY LIKE

- 1984 by George Orwell, ISBN: 9789380914947
- 12 Years a Slave by Solomon Northup, ISBN: 9789390492374
- 51 Most Powerful Prayers by Ryan, ISBN: 9789354990847
- A Christmas Carol by Charles Dickens, ISBN: 9788193545874
- A Cloud by Day, a Fire by Night by AW Tozer, ISBN: 9789354990854
- A Passage to India by E.M. Forster, ISBN: 9789354990205
- A Room of One's Own by Virginia Woolf, ISBN: 9789354990281
- A Streetcar Named Desire by Tennessee Williams, ISBN: 9788194748601
- A Wrinkle in Time by Madeleine L'Engle, ISBN: 9789354991066
- Abraham Lincoln by Lord Charnwood, ISBN: 9789380914251
- Absolute Surrender by Andrew Murray, ISBN: 9789389716269
- Animal Farm by George Orwell, ISBN: 9789380914701
- Anthem by Ayn Rand, ISBN: 9789389157079
- As a Man Thinketh by James Allen, ISBN: 9788180320262
- As I Lay Dying by William Faulkner, ISBN: 9789390492381
- Awakened Imagination by Neville Goddard, ISBN: 9789389157086
- Be What You Wish by Neville Goddard, ISBN: 9789387669550
- Chanakya Neeti by Chanakya, ISBN: 9789389716276
- Civilization and Its Discontents by Sigmund Freud, ISBN: 9789387669499
- Delighting in God by AW Tozer, ISBN: 9788194748632
- Demian by Hermann Hesse, ISBN: 9789387669567
- Experiencing the Holy Spirit by Andrew Murray, ISBN: 9788194764809
- Feeling is the Secret by Neville Goddard, ISBN: 9789389157109
- George Orwell Combo : Animal Farm & 1984, ISBN: 9789390492459
- Gravity by George Gamow, ISBN: 9789388118484
- Guerrilla Warfare by Ernesto Che Guevara, ISBN: 9789354990366

Develop your reading habit | **Gift books to your friends**

OTHER BOOKS YOU MAY LIKE

- How to be filled with the Holy Spirit by AW Tozer, ISBN: 9789389157116
- How to Develop Self Confidence by Dale Carnegie, ISBN: 9789387669000
- In His Steps by Charles M. Sheldon, ISBN: 9789390492794
- Life of Christ by Fulton J. Sheen, ISBN: 9789389716306
- Lost Horizon by James Hilton, ISBN: 9789389716313
- Man: The Dwelling Place of God by AW Tozer, ISBN: 9789354990656
- Maneaters of Kumaon by Jim Corbett, ISBN: 9789354990731
- Mansarover 1 (Hindi) by Premchand, ISBN: 9789380914978
- Mansarover 2 (Hindi) by Premchand, ISBN: 9789380914985
- Meditation and Its Methods by Swami Vivekananda, ISBN: 9789389716320
- One, None and a Hundred Thousand by Luigi Pirandello, ISBN: 9789389716337
- Paths to Power by AW Tozer, ISBN: Forthcoming
- Scientific Healing Affirmations by P. Yogananda, ISBN: 9789389716344
- Selected Stories of Rabindranath Tagore by Tagore, ISBN: 9789380914770
- Siddhartha by Hermann Hesse, ISBN: 9789380914145
- Student's Encyclopedia of G. K. by GP Editors, ISBN: 9789380914190
- Tales from Shakespeare by Charles Lamb & Mary Lamb, ISBN: 9789380914367
- The Alchemy of Happiness by Al-Ghazzali, ISBN: 9789387669505
- The Book of Enoch by Enoch, ISBN: 9789390492480
- The Dynamic Laws of Prosperity by Catherine Ponder, ISBN: 9789388118156
- The Game of Life and How to Play It by Florence Shinn, ISBN: 9789387669390
- The Imitation of Christ by Thomas À Kempis, ISBN: 9789388118057
- The Knowledge of the Holy by AW Tozer, ISBN: 9789389157130
- The Law by Neville Goddard, ISBN: 9789390492886
- The Light of Asia by Sir Edwin Arnold, ISBN: 9789380914923
- The Magic of Believing by Claude Bristol, ISBN: 9789388118149

Develop your reading habit | **Gift books to your friends**

OTHER BOOKS YOU MAY LIKE

- The Magic of Faith by Joseph Murphy, ISBN: 9789388118743
- The Miracles of Your Mind by Joseph Murphy, ISBN: 9788180320743
- The Mysterious Affair at Styles by Agatha Christie, ISBN: 9789390492510
- The Origin of Species by Charles Darwin, ISBN: 9788180320453
- The Plague by Albert Camus, ISBN: 9788194764892
- The Power of Awareness by Neville Goddard, ISBN: 9789387669406
- The Power of Positive Thinking by Norman Vincent Peale, ISBN: 9789388118569
- The Problem of Increasing Human Energy by Nikola Tesla, ISBN: 9789354990953
- The Prophet by Kahlil Gibran, ISBN: 9789380914022
- The Psychopathology of Everyday Life by Sigmund Freud, ISBN: 9789388118071
- The Pursuit of God by AW Tozer, ISBN: 9789389157147
- The Railway Children by E Nesbit, ISBN: 9789354990960
- The Red Badge of Courage by Stephen Crane, ISBN: 9789354990977
- The Sound and the Fury by William Faulkner, ISBN: 9789390492572
- The Stranger by Albert Camus, ISBN: 9789390492589
- The Sun Also Rises by Ernest Hemingway, ISBN: 9789354990984
- The Yoga Sutras of Patanjali by Patanjali, ISBN: 9789389716351
- Their Eyes Were Watching God by Zora Neale Hurston, ISBN: 9788194764885
- Think and Grow Rich by Napoleon Hill, ISBN: 9788180320255
- Thought Vibration by William Walker Atkinson, ISBN: 9789389157154
- To the Lighthouse by Virginia Woolf, ISBN: 9789390492190
- Who were the Shudras by Dr B.R. Ambedkar, ISBN: 9789354991028
- World's Best Short Stories: Volume 1 by Various Authors, ISBN: 9789390492275
- Wuthering Heights by Emily Brontë, ISBN: 9788193545898
- Your Faith is Your Fortune by Neville Goddard, ISBN: 9789389157161
- Zen in the Art of Archery by Eugen Herrigel, ISBN: 9789354991059

Develop your reading habit | Gift books to your friends

www.ingramcontent.com/pod-product-compliance
Ingram Content Group UK Ltd.
Pitfield, Milton Keynes, MK11 3LW, UK
UKHW032042260826
14628UKWH00008B/3130

9 789354 993893